feels grateful today

spiritual
FRUiT

JOURNALS

"Count Your Blessings" Section

I'M GRATEFUL FOR:

Take a few moments every day and write down three things that you are grateful for. Pray for a grateful heart and ask God to teach you to be joyful always and to help you to choose gratitude in all circumstances. Form the habit of writing in your journal daily to help you to cultivate a heart of gratitude and focus on the blessings in your life. *"Always be joyful. Never stop praying. Be thankful in all circumstances, for this is God's will for you who belong to Christ Jesus." - 1 Thessalonians 5:16-18, NLT*

count your
BLESSINGS

Be thankful in all circumstances, for this is God's will for you who belong to Christ Jesus.
- 1 THESSALONIANS 5:18, NLT

Date:

I'M GRATEFUL FOR:	HIGHLIGHT OF THE DAY:

Date:

I'M GRATEFUL FOR:	HIGHLIGHT OF THE DAY:

Date:

I'M GRATEFUL FOR:	HIGHLIGHT OF THE DAY:

Date:

I'M GRATEFUL FOR:	HIGHLIGHT OF THE DAY:

Date:

I'M GRATEFUL FOR:	HIGHLIGHT OF THE DAY:

Date:

I'M GRATEFUL FOR:	HIGHLIGHT OF THE DAY:

HIGHLIGHT OF THE DAY:

Capture the highlight of your day here. Reflect on a memorable moment or verse that inspired you, brightened your day and made you smile.

Weekly Reflection Section

The Weekly Reflection pages are placed immediately after each week of practicing gratitude and include simple guided activities designed to help you to reflect on your grateful moments from the previous week and to set goals for embracing an ongoing attitude of gratitude as a way of life.

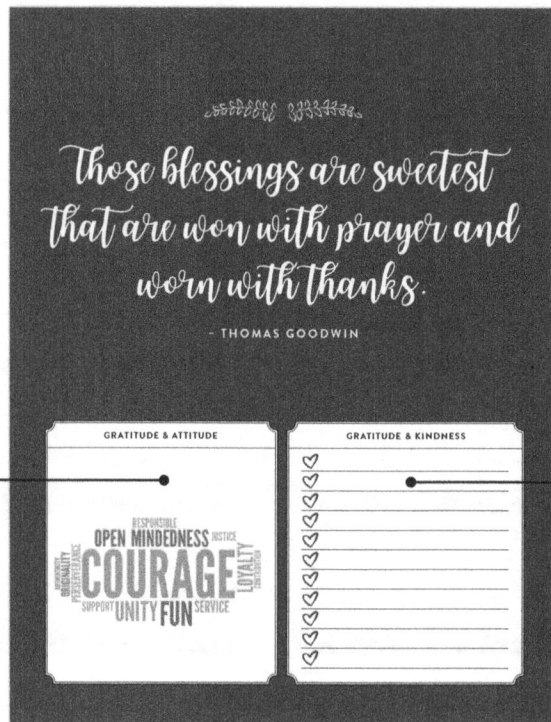

Those blessings are sweetest that are won with prayer and worn with thanks.

– THOMAS GOODWIN

GRATITUDE & ATTITUDE

Starting each day with a positive focus and a grateful heart may positively impact your mood and emotions, providing you with a new perspective on life. Using the block of words as a guide, circle or highlight the ones that best describe any noticeable shifts in your mindset, outlook or emotions after a consistent practice of gratitude. Add your own words and witness how a daily practice of gratitude and adopting a grateful and thankful attitude can affect your everyday emotions. Cultivate a heart of gratitude with daily prayers of thanksgiving and appreciation. *"Devote yourselves to prayer, keeping alert in it with an attitude of thanksgiving."*
- Colossians 4:2, NASB

GRATITUDE & KINDNESS

An attitude of gratitude may inspire you to act with kindness, or perhaps you might see an opportunity where you can "pay it forward." Reflect on the acts of kindness you performed over the previous week and consider how they impacted your life and others. Include some ways that you could be a kinder person and stretch beyond your comfort zone to perform a random act of kindness. *"Be kind to one another, tender-hearted, forgiving each other, just as God in Christ also has forgiven you."*
- Ephesians 4:32, NASB

MOST MEMORABLE MOMENTS (GRATITUDE JAR)

Collect last week's top moments and celebrations in the jar and witness all the good in your life pile up. *"O satisfy us in the morning with Your loving kindness, that we may sing for joy and be glad all our days." - Psalm 90:14, NASB*

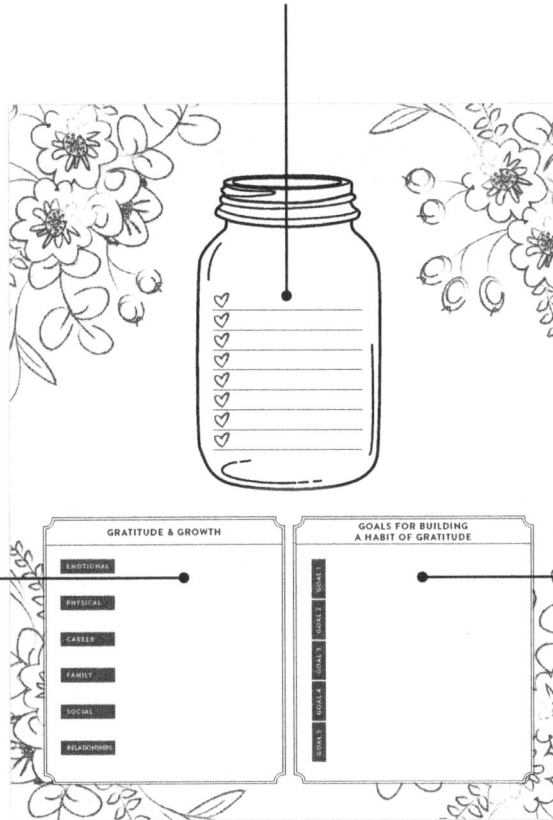

GRATITUDE & GROWTH

EMOTIONAL

PHYSICAL

CAREER

FAMILY

SOCIAL

RELATIONSHIPS

GOALS FOR BUILDING
A HABIT OF GRATITUDE

GOAL 1

GOAL 2

GOAL 3

GOAL 4

GOAL 5

GRATITUDE & GROWTH

There may be some areas in your life where you have realized growth and experienced positive benefits from a consistent practice of gratitude. Take some time to reflect on these areas, noting where you've noticed growth and how your life has been impacted by positive thinking. Remember to offer a prayer of thanksgiving and appreciation to God for each of these benefits. *"Sing and make music from your heart to the Lord, always giving thanks to God the Father for everything, in the name of our Lord Jesus Christ." - Ephesians 5:19-20, NIV*

GOALS FOR BUILDING A HABIT OF GRATITUDE

Being mindfully grateful and thankful for the blessings in your life can be a rewarding habit to practice. Set new personal goals and reflect on the ways that you intend to embrace an ongoing attitude of gratitude, reminding yourself to pause and be thankful for even the small things. Ask God to help you to discover the joy of a grateful heart and give you the ingredients for growing and cultivating a heart of gratitude. Try treating each day like a treasure hunt, always seeking grateful moments and giving thanks for the blessings you receive. *"May he give you the desire of your heart and make all your plans succeed." - Psalm 20:4, NIV*

count your
BLESSINGS

Be thankful in all circumstances, for this is God's will for you who belong to Christ Jesus.

– 1 THESSALONIANS 5:18, NLT

Date:

I'M GRATEFUL FOR:	HIGHLIGHT OF THE DAY:

Date:

I'M GRATEFUL FOR:	HIGHLIGHT OF THE DAY:

Date:

I'M GRATEFUL FOR:	HIGHLIGHT OF THE DAY:

Date:

I'M GRATEFUL FOR:	HIGHLIGHT OF THE DAY:

Date:

I'M GRATEFUL FOR:	HIGHLIGHT OF THE DAY:

Date:

I'M GRATEFUL FOR:	HIGHLIGHT OF THE DAY:

Date:

I'M GRATEFUL FOR:	HIGHLIGHT OF THE DAY:

Those blessings are sweetest that are won with prayer and worn with thanks.

– THOMAS GOODWIN

GRATITUDE & ATTITUDE

RESPONSIBLE
OPEN MINDEDNESS JUSTICE
AUTHENTICITY
ORIGINALITY
PERSERVERANCE
COURAGE LOYALTY
CONTRIBUTION
SUPPORT UNITY FUN SERVICE

GRATITUDE & KINDNESS

♡ _____
♡ _____
♡ _____
♡ _____
♡ _____
♡ _____
♡ _____
♡ _____
♡ _____
♡ _____

gratitude jar

♡ _____
♡ _____
♡ _____
♡ _____
♡ _____
♡ _____
♡ _____
♡ _____

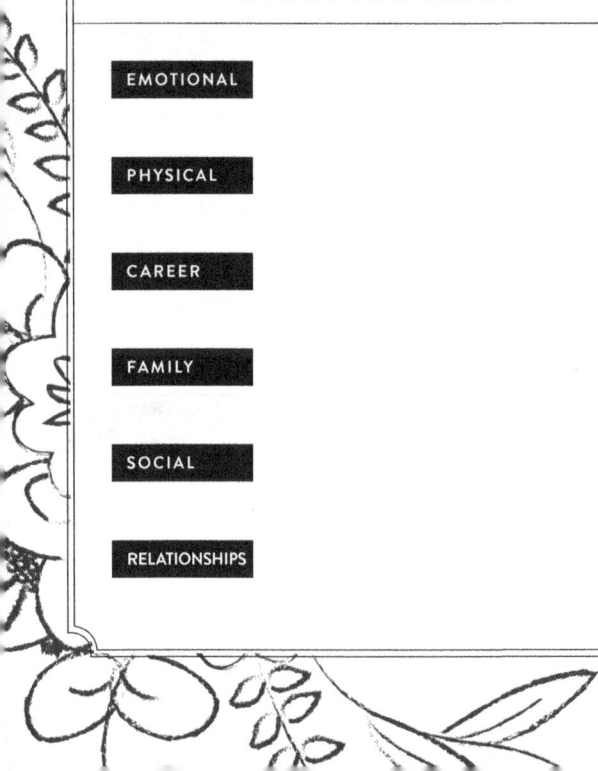

GRATITUDE & GROWTH

- EMOTIONAL
- PHYSICAL
- CAREER
- FAMILY
- SOCIAL
- RELATIONSHIPS

GOALS FOR BUILDING A HABIT OF GRATITUDE

- GOAL 1
- GOAL 2
- GOAL 3
- GOAL 4
- GOAL 5

count your

BLESSINGS

Trust in the Lord with all your heart and do not lean on your own understanding.
In all your ways acknowledge Him, and He will make your paths straight.

– PROVERBS 3:5-6, NASB

Date:

I'M GRATEFUL FOR:	HIGHLIGHT OF THE DAY:

Date:

I'M GRATEFUL FOR:	HIGHLIGHT OF THE DAY:

Date:

I'M GRATEFUL FOR:	HIGHLIGHT OF THE DAY:

Date:

I'M GRATEFUL FOR:	HIGHLIGHT OF THE DAY:

Date:

I'M GRATEFUL FOR:	HIGHLIGHT OF THE DAY:

Date:

I'M GRATEFUL FOR:	HIGHLIGHT OF THE DAY:

Date:

I'M GRATEFUL FOR:	HIGHLIGHT OF THE DAY:

A state of mind that sees God in everything is evidence of growth in grace and a thankful heart.

— CHARLES G. FINNEY

GRATITUDE & ATTITUDE

LEARNING LEAD SENSITIVITY GRATITUDE
ADVENTURE CONTENTMENT ACCEPTANCE GROWTH PACIFIST DREAM SPONTANEOUS INTUITION
COMPASSION INTIMACY HONESTY LISTENING HOPE DEVOTION
GENEROSITY FREEDOM WEALTH ACCEPTANCE BEAUTY FAIRNESS
COMMUNITY DEPENDABLE FRIENDLINESS

GRATITUDE & KINDNESS

♡ _____
♡ _____
♡ _____
♡ _____
♡ _____
♡ _____
♡ _____
♡ _____
♡ _____
♡ _____
♡ _____
♡ _____

gratitude jar

- ♡ _____
- ♡ _____
- ♡ _____
- ♡ _____
- ♡ _____
- ♡ _____
- ♡ _____
- ♡ _____

GRATITUDE & GROWTH

- **EMOTIONAL**
- **PHYSICAL**
- **CAREER**
- **FAMILY**
- **SOCIAL**
- **RELATIONSHIPS**

GOALS FOR BUILDING A HABIT OF GRATITUDE

- **GOAL 1**
- **GOAL 2**
- **GOAL 3**
- **GOAL 4**
- **GOAL 5**

count your
BLESSINGS

But the fruit of the Spirit is love, joy, peace, patience, kindness, goodness, faithfulness, gentleness, self-control; against such things there is no law.

– GALATIANS 5:22-23, NASB

Date:

I'M GRATEFUL FOR:	HIGHLIGHT OF THE DAY:

Date:

I'M GRATEFUL FOR:	HIGHLIGHT OF THE DAY:

Date:

I'M GRATEFUL FOR:	HIGHLIGHT OF THE DAY:

Date:

I'M GRATEFUL FOR:	HIGHLIGHT OF THE DAY:

Date:

I'M GRATEFUL FOR:	HIGHLIGHT OF THE DAY:

Date:

I'M GRATEFUL FOR:	HIGHLIGHT OF THE DAY:

Date:

I'M GRATEFUL FOR:	HIGHLIGHT OF THE DAY:

Careful for nothing, prayerful for everything, thankful for anything.

– DWIGHT LYMAN MOODY

GRATITUDE & ATTITUDE

SELF DEVELOPMENT
SELF RELIANCE
BALANCE
LOVE
CREATIVITY
ATTENTIVE
NURTURING
RELIABLE
SECURITY
POSITIVITY
HEALTH
GRACE
FAMILY
IDEALISM
FAITH
RISK TAKING
ENTHUSIASM
INSPIRATION
CONNECTION
TRUSTWORTHINESS

GRATITUDE & KINDNESS

♡ _____
♡ _____
♡ _____
♡ _____
♡ _____
♡ _____
♡ _____
♡ _____
♡ _____
♡ _____
♡ _____

gratitude jar

♡ _____
♡ _____
♡ _____
♡ _____
♡ _____
♡ _____
♡ _____
♡ _____

GRATITUDE & GROWTH

EMOTIONAL

PHYSICAL

CAREER

FAMILY

SOCIAL

RELATIONSHIPS

GOALS FOR BUILDING
A HABIT OF GRATITUDE

GOAL 1

GOAL 2

GOAL 3

GOAL 4

GOAL 5

count your
BLESSINGS

Ask and it will be given to you; seek and you will find; knock and the door will be opened to you. For everyone who asks receives; the one who seeks finds; and to the one who knocks, the door will be opened.

– MATTHEW 7:7-9, NIV

Date:

I'M GRATEFUL FOR:	HIGHLIGHT OF THE DAY:

Date:

I'M GRATEFUL FOR:	HIGHLIGHT OF THE DAY:

Date:

I'M GRATEFUL FOR:	HIGHLIGHT OF THE DAY:

Date:

I'M GRATEFUL FOR:	HIGHLIGHT OF THE DAY:

Date:

I'M GRATEFUL FOR:	HIGHLIGHT OF THE DAY:

Date:

I'M GRATEFUL FOR:	HIGHLIGHT OF THE DAY:

Date:

I'M GRATEFUL FOR:	HIGHLIGHT OF THE DAY:

God bless the good-natured, for they bless everybody else.

– HENRY WARD BEECHER

GRATITUDE & ATTITUDE

IMAGINATION DEDICATION HUMUOR UNDERSTANDING INTEGRITY PEACEFUL CONTROL WISDOM HAPPINESS SUCCESS PLAYFULNESS INTENTIONAL DISCIPLINED INVENTIVE EQUALITY CONNECTION ENDURANCE LAUGHTER PATIENCE AWARENESS

GRATITUDE & KINDNESS

- ♡ _____
- ♡ _____
- ♡ _____
- ♡ _____
- ♡ _____
- ♡ _____
- ♡ _____
- ♡ _____
- ♡ _____
- ♡ _____
- ♡ _____

gratitude jar

♡ _____
♡ _____
♡ _____
♡ _____
♡ _____
♡ _____
♡ _____
♡ _____

GRATITUDE & GROWTH

EMOTIONAL

PHYSICAL

CAREER

FAMILY

SOCIAL

RELATIONSHIPS

GOALS FOR BUILDING A HABIT OF GRATITUDE

GOAL 1

GOAL 2

GOAL 3

GOAL 4

GOAL 5

BLESSINGS

Sing to the Lord with grateful praise;
make music to our God on the harp.

— PSALM 147:7, NIV

Date:

I'M GRATEFUL FOR:	HIGHLIGHT OF THE DAY:

Date:

I'M GRATEFUL FOR:	HIGHLIGHT OF THE DAY:

Date:

I'M GRATEFUL FOR:	HIGHLIGHT OF THE DAY:

Date:

I'M GRATEFUL FOR:	HIGHLIGHT OF THE DAY:

Date:

I'M GRATEFUL FOR:	HIGHLIGHT OF THE DAY:

Date:

I'M GRATEFUL FOR:	HIGHLIGHT OF THE DAY:

Date:

I'M GRATEFUL FOR:	HIGHLIGHT OF THE DAY:

You must keep all earthy treasures out of your heart, and let Christ be your treasure, and let Him have your heart.

– CHARLES SPURGEON

GRATITUDE & ATTITUDE

RESPONSIBLE
OPEN MINDEDNESS JUSTICE
AUTHENTICITY
ORIGINALITY
PERSEVERANCE
COURAGE LOYALTY
CONTRIBUTION
SUPPORT UNITY FUN SERVICE

GRATITUDE & KINDNESS

- ♡ _____
- ♡ _____
- ♡ _____
- ♡ _____
- ♡ _____
- ♡ _____
- ♡ _____
- ♡ _____
- ♡ _____
- ♡ _____
- ♡ _____

gratitude jar

- ♡ _____
- ♡ _____
- ♡ _____
- ♡ _____
- ♡ _____
- ♡ _____
- ♡ _____
- ♡ _____

GRATITUDE & GROWTH

- EMOTIONAL
- PHYSICAL
- CAREER
- FAMILY
- SOCIAL
- RELATIONSHIPS

GOALS FOR BUILDING A HABIT OF GRATITUDE

- GOAL 1
- GOAL 2
- GOAL 3
- GOAL 4
- GOAL 5

count your
BLESSINGS

I will give thanks to the Lord because of his righteousness;
I will sing the praises of the name of the Lord Most High.

– PSALM 7:17, NIV

Date:

I'M GRATEFUL FOR:	HIGHLIGHT OF THE DAY:

Date:

I'M GRATEFUL FOR:	HIGHLIGHT OF THE DAY:

Date:

I'M GRATEFUL FOR:	HIGHLIGHT OF THE DAY:

Date:

I'M GRATEFUL FOR:	HIGHLIGHT OF THE DAY:

Date:

I'M GRATEFUL FOR:	HIGHLIGHT OF THE DAY:

Date:

I'M GRATEFUL FOR:	HIGHLIGHT OF THE DAY:

Date:

I'M GRATEFUL FOR:	HIGHLIGHT OF THE DAY:

Our God is so wonderfully good, and lovely, and blessed in every way that the mere fact of belonging to Him is enough for an untellable fullness of joy!

– HANNAH WHITALL SMITH

GRATITUDE & ATTITUDE

LEARNING LEAD SENSITIVITY GRATITUDE
ADVENTURE CONTENTMENT GROWTH PACIFIST DREAM
COMPASSION ACCEPTANCE SPONTANEOUS INTUITION
GENEROSITY INTIMACY HONESTY LISTENING CONTENTMENT HOPE DEVOTION
FREEDOM COMMUNITY DEPENDABLE WEALTH ACCEPTANCE BEAUTY FAIRNESS
FRIENDLINESS

GRATITUDE & KINDNESS

♡ _____
♡ _____
♡ _____
♡ _____
♡ _____
♡ _____
♡ _____
♡ _____
♡ _____
♡ _____
♡ _____

gratitude jar

- ♡ _____
- ♡ _____
- ♡ _____
- ♡ _____
- ♡ _____
- ♡ _____
- ♡ _____
- ♡ _____

GRATITUDE & GROWTH

- EMOTIONAL
- PHYSICAL
- CAREER
- FAMILY
- SOCIAL
- RELATIONSHIPS

GOALS FOR BUILDING A HABIT OF GRATITUDE

- GOAL 1
- GOAL 2
- GOAL 3
- GOAL 4
- GOAL 5

count your
BLESSINGS

Be careful for nothing; but in every thing by prayer and supplication with thanksgiving let your requests be made known unto God.

– PHILIPPIANS 4:6, KJV

Date:

I'M GRATEFUL FOR:	HIGHLIGHT OF THE DAY:

Date:

I'M GRATEFUL FOR:	HIGHLIGHT OF THE DAY:

Date:

I'M GRATEFUL FOR:	HIGHLIGHT OF THE DAY:

Date:

I'M GRATEFUL FOR:	HIGHLIGHT OF THE DAY:

Date:

I'M GRATEFUL FOR:	HIGHLIGHT OF THE DAY:

Date:

I'M GRATEFUL FOR:	HIGHLIGHT OF THE DAY:

Date:

I'M GRATEFUL FOR:	HIGHLIGHT OF THE DAY:

Kind words do not cost much. Yet they accomplish much.

– BLAISE PASCAL

GRATITUDE & ATTITUDE

SELF DEVELOPMENT
SELF RELIANCE
BALANCE ATTENTIVE
LOVE CREATIVITY RELIABLE SECURITY
IDEALISM POSITIVITY
HEALTH GRACE NURTURING FAITH RISK TAKING ENTHUSIASM
FAMILY INSPIRATION CONNECTION
TRUSTWORTHINESS

GRATITUDE & KINDNESS

gratitude jar

♡ _____
♡ _____
♡ _____
♡ _____
♡ _____
♡ _____
♡ _____
♡ _____

GRATITUDE & GROWTH

EMOTIONAL

PHYSICAL

CAREER

FAMILY

SOCIAL

RELATIONSHIPS

GOALS FOR BUILDING
A HABIT OF GRATITUDE

GOAL 1

GOAL 2

GOAL 3

GOAL 4

GOAL 5

count your
BLESSINGS

This is the day the Lord has made.
We will rejoice and be glad in it.

– PSALM 118:24, NLT

Date:

I'M GRATEFUL FOR:	HIGHLIGHT OF THE DAY:

Date:

I'M GRATEFUL FOR:	HIGHLIGHT OF THE DAY:

Date:

I'M GRATEFUL FOR:	HIGHLIGHT OF THE DAY:

Date:

I'M GRATEFUL FOR:	HIGHLIGHT OF THE DAY:

Date:

I'M GRATEFUL FOR:	HIGHLIGHT OF THE DAY:

Date:

I'M GRATEFUL FOR:	HIGHLIGHT OF THE DAY:

Date:

I'M GRATEFUL FOR:	HIGHLIGHT OF THE DAY:

The unthankful heart discovers no mercies; but let the thankful heart sweep through the day and, as the magnet finds the iron, so it will find, in every hour, some heavenly blessings!

– HENRY WARD BEECHER

GRATITUDE & ATTITUDE

UNDERSTANDING INTEGRITY
HUMUOR
DEDICATION HAPPINESS SUCCESS PEACEFUL CONTROL WISDOM
IMAGINATION INTENTIONAL DISCIPLINED INVENTIVE
PLAYFULNESS
EQUALITY CONNECTION ENDURANCE
PATIENCE AWARENESS LAUGHTER

GRATITUDE & KINDNESS

gratitude jar

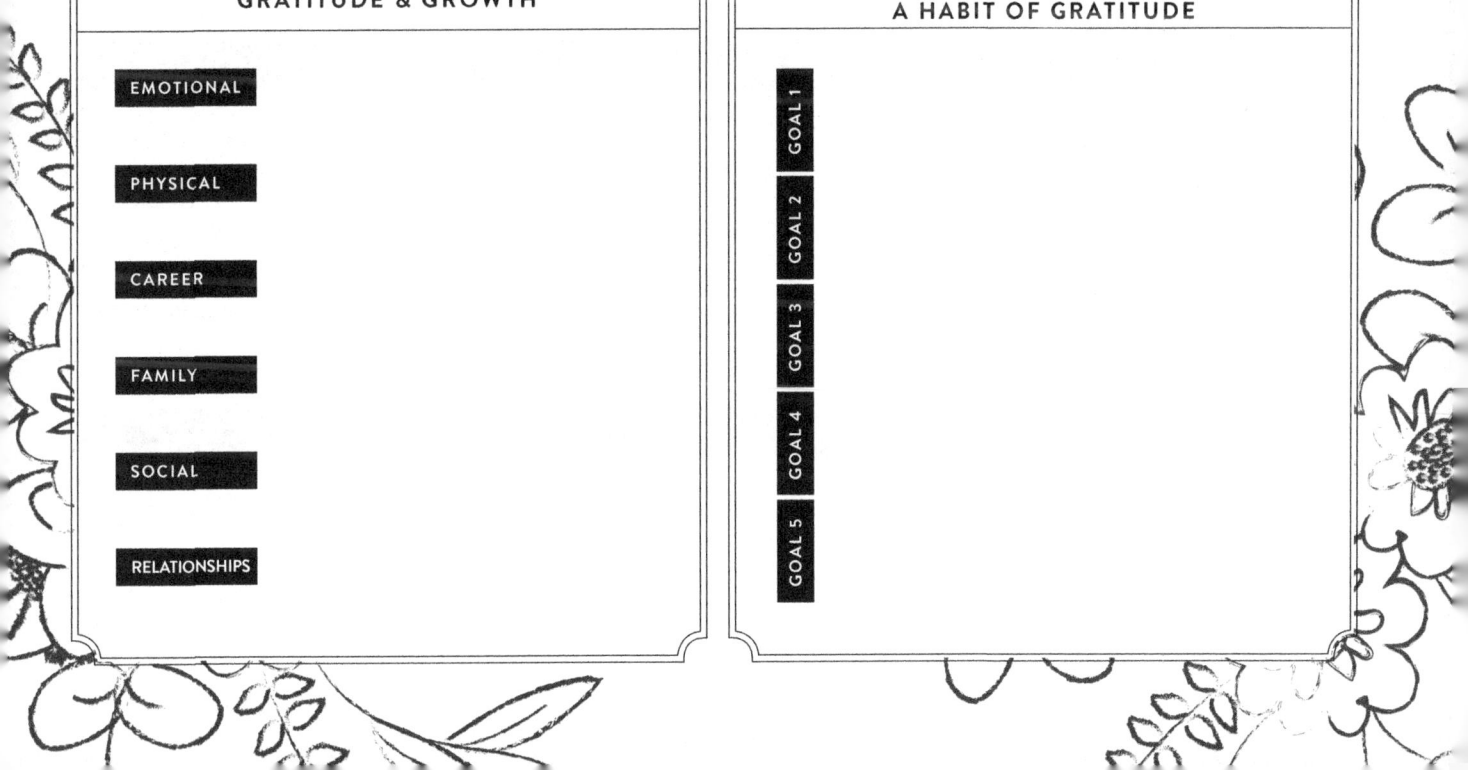

GRATITUDE & GROWTH

EMOTIONAL

PHYSICAL

CAREER

FAMILY

SOCIAL

RELATIONSHIPS

GOALS FOR BUILDING
A HABIT OF GRATITUDE

GOAL 1

GOAL 2

GOAL 3

GOAL 4

GOAL 5

count your

BLESSINGS

O give thanks unto the Lord; for he is good: for his mercy endureth for ever.

— PSALM 136:1, KJV

Date:

I'M GRATEFUL FOR:	HIGHLIGHT OF THE DAY:

Date:

I'M GRATEFUL FOR:	HIGHLIGHT OF THE DAY:

Date:

I'M GRATEFUL FOR:	HIGHLIGHT OF THE DAY:

Date:

I'M GRATEFUL FOR:	HIGHLIGHT OF THE DAY:

Date:

I'M GRATEFUL FOR:	HIGHLIGHT OF THE DAY:

Date:

I'M GRATEFUL FOR:	HIGHLIGHT OF THE DAY:

Date:

I'M GRATEFUL FOR:	HIGHLIGHT OF THE DAY:

After a storm comes a calm.

– MATTHEW HENRY

GRATITUDE & ATTITUDE

RESPONSIBLE
OPEN MINDEDNESS JUSTICE
AUTHENTICITY
ORIGINALITY
PERSERVERANCE
COURAGE LOYALTY
CONTRIBUTION
SUPPORT UNITY FUN SERVICE

GRATITUDE & KINDNESS

♡ _____
♡ _____
♡ _____
♡ _____
♡ _____
♡ _____
♡ _____
♡ _____
♡ _____
♡ _____
♡ _____

gratitude jar

♡ _____
♡ _____
♡ _____
♡ _____
♡ _____
♡ _____
♡ _____
♡ _____

GRATITUDE & GROWTH

- EMOTIONAL
- PHYSICAL
- CAREER
- FAMILY
- SOCIAL
- RELATIONSHIPS

GOALS FOR BUILDING A HABIT OF GRATITUDE

- GOAL 1
- GOAL 2
- GOAL 3
- GOAL 4
- GOAL 5

count your
BLESSINGS

"For I know the plans I have for you," says the Lord. "They are plans for good and not for disaster, to give you a future and a hope."

-JEREMIAH 29:11, NLT

Date:

I'M GRATEFUL FOR:	HIGHLIGHT OF THE DAY:

Date:

I'M GRATEFUL FOR:	HIGHLIGHT OF THE DAY:

Date:

I'M GRATEFUL FOR:	HIGHLIGHT OF THE DAY:

Date:

I'M GRATEFUL FOR:	HIGHLIGHT OF THE DAY:

Date:

I'M GRATEFUL FOR:	HIGHLIGHT OF THE DAY:

Date:

I'M GRATEFUL FOR:	HIGHLIGHT OF THE DAY:

Date:

I'M GRATEFUL FOR:	HIGHLIGHT OF THE DAY:

Seek to cultivate a buoyant, joyous sense of the crowded kindnesses of God in your daily life.

– ALEXANDER MACLAREN

GRATITUDE & ATTITUDE

GRATITUDE
LEARNING LEAD SENSITIVITY
ADVENTURE CONTENTMENT GRATITUDE GROWTH PACIFIST DREAM
COMPASSION ACCEPTANCE SPONTANEOUS INTUITION
GENEROSITY FREEDOM INTIMACY LISTENING HOPE DEVOTION
COMMUNITY HONESTY BEAUTY FAIRNESS
DEPENDABLE WEALTH
FRIENDLINESS

GRATITUDE & KINDNESS

♡ _____
♡ _____
♡ _____
♡ _____
♡ _____
♡ _____
♡ _____
♡ _____
♡ _____
♡ _____
♡ _____

gratitude jar

♡ _____
♡ _____
♡ _____
♡ _____
♡ _____
♡ _____
♡ _____
♡ _____

GRATITUDE & GROWTH

EMOTIONAL

PHYSICAL

CAREER

FAMILY

SOCIAL

RELATIONSHIPS

GOALS FOR BUILDING A HABIT OF GRATITUDE

GOAL 1

GOAL 2

GOAL 3

GOAL 4

GOAL 5

count your
BLESSINGS

Sing praise to the Lord, you His godly ones,
and give thanks to His holy name.

– PSALM 30:4, NASB

Date:

I'M GRATEFUL FOR:	HIGHLIGHT OF THE DAY:

Date:

I'M GRATEFUL FOR:	HIGHLIGHT OF THE DAY:

Date:

I'M GRATEFUL FOR:	HIGHLIGHT OF THE DAY:

Date:

I'M GRATEFUL FOR:	HIGHLIGHT OF THE DAY:

Date:

I'M GRATEFUL FOR:	HIGHLIGHT OF THE DAY:

Date:

I'M GRATEFUL FOR:	HIGHLIGHT OF THE DAY:

Date:

I'M GRATEFUL FOR:	HIGHLIGHT OF THE DAY:

Be intent on the perfection of the present day.

– WILLIAM LAW

GRATITUDE & ATTITUDE

BALANCE
LOVE
HEALTH GRACE
FAMILY
SELF DEVELOPMENT
CREATIVITY
NURTURING
IDEALISM
NURTURING
SELF RELIANCE
ATTENTIVE
RESILIENCE
RELIABLE
SECURITY
POSITIVITY
FAITH
RISK TAKING
ENTHUSIASM
INSPIRATION
CONNECTION
TRUSTWORTHINESS

GRATITUDE & KINDNESS

♡ _____
♡ _____
♡ _____
♡ _____
♡ _____
♡ _____
♡ _____
♡ _____
♡ _____
♡ _____
♡ _____

gratitude jar

♡ _____
♡ _____
♡ _____
♡ _____
♡ _____
♡ _____
♡ _____
♡ _____

GRATITUDE & GROWTH

EMOTIONAL

PHYSICAL

CAREER

FAMILY

SOCIAL

RELATIONSHIPS

GOALS FOR BUILDING
A HABIT OF GRATITUDE

GOAL 1

GOAL 2

GOAL 3

GOAL 4

GOAL 5

count your
BLESSINGS

Do not be anxious about anything, but in every situation, by prayer and petition, with thanksgiving, present your requests to God. And the peace of God, which transcends all understanding, will guard your hearts and your minds in Christ Jesus.

-PHILIPPIANS 4:6-7, NIV

Date:

I'M GRATEFUL FOR:	HIGHLIGHT OF THE DAY:

Date:

I'M GRATEFUL FOR:	HIGHLIGHT OF THE DAY:

Date:

I'M GRATEFUL FOR:	HIGHLIGHT OF THE DAY:

Date:

I'M GRATEFUL FOR:	HIGHLIGHT OF THE DAY:

Date:

I'M GRATEFUL FOR:	HIGHLIGHT OF THE DAY:

Date:

I'M GRATEFUL FOR:	HIGHLIGHT OF THE DAY:

Date:

I'M GRATEFUL FOR:	HIGHLIGHT OF THE DAY:

Forget yourself and live for others, for it is more blessed to give than to receive.

— A.B. SIMPSON

GRATITUDE & ATTITUDE

RESPONSIBLE
OPEN MINDEDNESS JUSTICE
AUTHENTICITY
ORIGINALITY
PERSERVERANCE
COURAGE LOYALTY CONTRIBUTION
SUPPORT UNITY FUN SERVICE

GRATITUDE & KINDNESS

♡ _____
♡ _____
♡ _____
♡ _____
♡ _____
♡ _____
♡ _____
♡ _____
♡ _____
♡ _____
♡ _____

gratitude jar

- ♥ _____
- ♥ _____
- ♥ _____
- ♥ _____
- ♥ _____
- ♥ _____
- ♥ _____
- ♥ _____

GRATITUDE & GROWTH

- EMOTIONAL
- PHYSICAL
- CAREER
- FAMILY
- SOCIAL
- RELATIONSHIPS

GOALS FOR BUILDING A HABIT OF GRATITUDE

- GOAL 1
- GOAL 2
- GOAL 3
- GOAL 4
- GOAL 5

count your
BLESSINGS

Thanks be unto God for his unspeakable gift.

– 2 CORINTHIANS 9:15, KJV

Date:

I'M GRATEFUL FOR:	HIGHLIGHT OF THE DAY:

Date:

I'M GRATEFUL FOR:	HIGHLIGHT OF THE DAY:

Date:

I'M GRATEFUL FOR:	HIGHLIGHT OF THE DAY:

Date:

I'M GRATEFUL FOR:	HIGHLIGHT OF THE DAY:

Date:

I'M GRATEFUL FOR:	HIGHLIGHT OF THE DAY:

Date:

I'M GRATEFUL FOR:	HIGHLIGHT OF THE DAY:

Date:

I'M GRATEFUL FOR:	HIGHLIGHT OF THE DAY:

Kindness is the noblest weapon to conquer with.

— THOMAS FULLER

GRATITUDE & ATTITUDE

GRATITUDE
LEARNING LEAD SENSITIVITY
ADVENTURE CONTENTMENT GROWTH PACIFIST DREAM SPONTANEOUS INTUITION
COMPASSION ACCEPTANCE
GENEROSITY FREEDOM INTIMACY HONESTY LISTENING HOPE DEVOTION
COMMUNITY DEPENDABLE WEALTH CONTENTMENT BEAUTY FAIRNESS
FRIENDLINESS

GRATITUDE & KINDNESS

♡ _____
♡ _____
♡ _____
♡ _____
♡ _____
♡ _____
♡ _____
♡ _____
♡ _____
♡ _____
♡ _____

gratitude jar

- ♡ _____
- ♡ _____
- ♡ _____
- ♡ _____
- ♡ _____
- ♡ _____
- ♡ _____
- ♡ _____

GRATITUDE & GROWTH

- **EMOTIONAL**
- **PHYSICAL**
- **CAREER**
- **FAMILY**
- **SOCIAL**
- **RELATIONSHIPS**

GOALS FOR BUILDING
A HABIT OF GRATITUDE

- **GOAL 1**
- **GOAL 2**
- **GOAL 3**
- **GOAL 4**
- **GOAL 5**

count your
BLESSINGS

Devote yourselves to prayer,
being watchful and thankful.

– COLOSSIANS 4:2, NIV

Date:

I'M GRATEFUL FOR:	HIGHLIGHT OF THE DAY:

Date:

I'M GRATEFUL FOR:	HIGHLIGHT OF THE DAY:

Date:

I'M GRATEFUL FOR:	HIGHLIGHT OF THE DAY:

Date:

I'M GRATEFUL FOR:	HIGHLIGHT OF THE DAY:

Date:

I'M GRATEFUL FOR:	HIGHLIGHT OF THE DAY:

Date:

I'M GRATEFUL FOR:	HIGHLIGHT OF THE DAY:

Date:

I'M GRATEFUL FOR:	HIGHLIGHT OF THE DAY:

The greatest and best talent that God gives to any man or woman in this world is the talent of prayer.

– ALEXANDER WHYTE

GRATITUDE & ATTITUDE

SELF DEVELOPMENT
SELF RELIANCE
BALANCE
ATTENTIVE
LOVE
CREATIVITY
NURTURING
RESILIENCE
RELIABLE
SECURITY
POSITIVITY
IDEALISM
HEALTH
GRACE
FAMILY
NURTURING
FAITH
RISK TAKING
ENTHUSIASM
INSPIRATION
CONNECTION
TRUSTWORTHINESS

GRATITUDE & KINDNESS

gratitude jar

♡ _____
♡ _____
♡ _____
♡ _____
♡ _____
♡ _____
♡ _____
♡ _____

GRATITUDE & GROWTH

EMOTIONAL

PHYSICAL

CAREER

FAMILY

SOCIAL

RELATIONSHIPS

GOALS FOR BUILDING A HABIT OF GRATITUDE

GOAL 1

GOAL 2

GOAL 3

GOAL 4

GOAL 5

count your

BLESSINGS

*Give thanks to the Lord and proclaim his greatness.
Let the whole world know what he has done.*

– 1 CHRONICLES 16:8, NLT

Date:

I'M GRATEFUL FOR:	HIGHLIGHT OF THE DAY:

Date:

I'M GRATEFUL FOR:	HIGHLIGHT OF THE DAY:

Date:

I'M GRATEFUL FOR:	HIGHLIGHT OF THE DAY:

Date:

I'M GRATEFUL FOR:	HIGHLIGHT OF THE DAY:

Date:

I'M GRATEFUL FOR:	HIGHLIGHT OF THE DAY:

Date:

I'M GRATEFUL FOR:	HIGHLIGHT OF THE DAY:

Date:

I'M GRATEFUL FOR:	HIGHLIGHT OF THE DAY:

Put together all the tenderest love you know of, multiply it by infinity, and you will begin to see glimpses of the love and grace of God.

– HANNAH WHITALL SMITH

GRATITUDE & ATTITUDE

UNDERSTANDING INTEGRITY
HUMUOR PEACEFUL WISDOM
DEDICATION HAPPINESS SUCCESS CONTROL
IMAGINATION INTENTIONAL DISCIPLINED INVENTIVE
PLAYFULNESS ENDURANCE
EQUALITY CONNECTION LAUGHTER
PATIENCE AWARENESS

GRATITUDE & KINDNESS

gratitude jar

♡ _____
♡ _____
♡ _____
♡ _____
♡ _____
♡ _____
♡ _____
♡ _____

GRATITUDE & GROWTH

EMOTIONAL

PHYSICAL

CAREER

FAMILY

SOCIAL

RELATIONSHIPS

GOALS FOR BUILDING
A HABIT OF GRATITUDE

GOAL 1

GOAL 2

GOAL 3

GOAL 4

GOAL 5

count your
BLESSINGS

Now may the God of hope fill you with all joy and peace in believing, so that you will abound in hope by the power of the Holy Spirit.

– ROMANS 15:13, NASB

Date:

I'M GRATEFUL FOR:	HIGHLIGHT OF THE DAY:

Date:

I'M GRATEFUL FOR:	HIGHLIGHT OF THE DAY:

Date:

I'M GRATEFUL FOR:	HIGHLIGHT OF THE DAY:

Date:

I'M GRATEFUL FOR:	HIGHLIGHT OF THE DAY:

Date:

I'M GRATEFUL FOR:	HIGHLIGHT OF THE DAY:

Date:

I'M GRATEFUL FOR:	HIGHLIGHT OF THE DAY:

Date:

I'M GRATEFUL FOR:	HIGHLIGHT OF THE DAY:

The greatest saint in the world is not he who prays most or fasts most; it is not he who gives alms, or is most eminent for temperance, chastity or justice. It is he who is most thankful to God.

– WILLIAM LAW

GRATITUDE & ATTITUDE

RESPONSIBLE
OPEN MINDEDNESS JUSTICE
AUTHENTICITY
ORIGINALITY
PERSERVERANCE
COURAGE LOYALTY
CONTRIBUTION
SUPPORT UNITY FUN SERVICE

GRATITUDE & KINDNESS

gratitude jar

♡ _____
♡ _____
♡ _____
♡ _____
♡ _____
♡ _____
♡ _____
♡ _____

GRATITUDE & GROWTH

EMOTIONAL

PHYSICAL

CAREER

FAMILY

SOCIAL

RELATIONSHIPS

GOALS FOR BUILDING
A HABIT OF GRATITUDE

GOAL 1

GOAL 2

GOAL 3

GOAL 4

GOAL 5

count your
BLESSINGS

And let the peace that comes from Christ rule in your hearts. For as members of one body you are called to live in peace. And always be thankful.

– COLOSSIANS 3:15, NLT

Date:

I'M GRATEFUL FOR:	HIGHLIGHT OF THE DAY:

Date:

I'M GRATEFUL FOR:	HIGHLIGHT OF THE DAY:

Date:

I'M GRATEFUL FOR:	HIGHLIGHT OF THE DAY:

Date:

I'M GRATEFUL FOR:	HIGHLIGHT OF THE DAY:

Date:

I'M GRATEFUL FOR:	HIGHLIGHT OF THE DAY:

Date:

I'M GRATEFUL FOR:	HIGHLIGHT OF THE DAY:

Date:

I'M GRATEFUL FOR:	HIGHLIGHT OF THE DAY:

Anything is a blessing which makes us pray.

– CHARLES SPURGEON

GRATITUDE & ATTITUDE

GRATITUDE
LEARNING LEAD SENSITIVITY
ADVENTURE CONTENTMENT ACCEPTANCE GROWTH PACIFIST DREAM SPONTANEOUS INTUITION
COMPASSION CONTENTMENT ACCEPTANCE HOPE DEVOTION
GENEROSITY FREEDOM INTIMACY LISTENING BEAUTY FAIRNESS
COMMUNITY DEPENDABLE WEALTH FRIENDLINESS

GRATITUDE & KINDNESS

♡ _____
♡ _____
♡ _____
♡ _____
♡ _____
♡ _____
♡ _____
♡ _____
♡ _____
♡ _____
♡ _____

gratitude jar

♡ _____
♡ _____
♡ _____
♡ _____
♡ _____
♡ _____
♡ _____
♡ _____

GRATITUDE & GROWTH

EMOTIONAL

PHYSICAL

CAREER

FAMILY

SOCIAL

RELATIONSHIPS

GOALS FOR BUILDING
A HABIT OF GRATITUDE

GOAL 1

GOAL 2

GOAL 3

GOAL 4

GOAL 5

count your
BLESSINGS

That I may proclaim with the voice of thanksgiving and declare all Your wonders.

– PSALM 26:7, NASB

Date:

I'M GRATEFUL FOR:	HIGHLIGHT OF THE DAY:

Date:

I'M GRATEFUL FOR:	HIGHLIGHT OF THE DAY:

Date:

I'M GRATEFUL FOR:	HIGHLIGHT OF THE DAY:

Date:

I'M GRATEFUL FOR:	HIGHLIGHT OF THE DAY:

Date:

I'M GRATEFUL FOR:	HIGHLIGHT OF THE DAY:

Date:

I'M GRATEFUL FOR:	HIGHLIGHT OF THE DAY:

Date:

I'M GRATEFUL FOR:	HIGHLIGHT OF THE DAY:

Gratitude is the fairest blossom which springs from the soul.

– HENRY WARD BEECHER

GRATITUDE & ATTITUDE

SELF DEVELOPMENT
SELF RELIANCE
BALANCE
ATTENTIVE
LOVE
IDEALISM
CREATIVITY
RELIABLE
SECURITY
POSITIVITY
NURTURING
NURTURING RESILIENCE
FAITH
RISK TAKING
ENTHUSIASM
HEALTH
GRACE
FAMILY
INSPIRATION
CONNECTION
TRUSTWORTHINESS

GRATITUDE & KINDNESS

♡ _____
♡ _____
♡ _____
♡ _____
♡ _____
♡ _____
♡ _____
♡ _____
♡ _____
♡ _____
♡ _____

gratitude jar

♡ _____
♡ _____
♡ _____
♡ _____
♡ _____
♡ _____
♡ _____
♡ _____

GRATITUDE & GROWTH

EMOTIONAL

PHYSICAL

CAREER

FAMILY

SOCIAL

RELATIONSHIPS

GOALS FOR BUILDING
A HABIT OF GRATITUDE

GOAL 1

GOAL 2

GOAL 3

GOAL 4

GOAL 5

count your
BLESSINGS

And whatever you do, whether in word or deed, do it all in the name of the Lord Jesus, giving thanks to God the Father through him.

– COLOSSIANS 3:17, NIV

Date:

I'M GRATEFUL FOR:	HIGHLIGHT OF THE DAY:

Date:

I'M GRATEFUL FOR:	HIGHLIGHT OF THE DAY:

Date:

I'M GRATEFUL FOR:	HIGHLIGHT OF THE DAY:

Date:

I'M GRATEFUL FOR:	HIGHLIGHT OF THE DAY:

Date:

I'M GRATEFUL FOR:	HIGHLIGHT OF THE DAY:

Date:

I'M GRATEFUL FOR:	HIGHLIGHT OF THE DAY:

Date:

I'M GRATEFUL FOR:	HIGHLIGHT OF THE DAY:

When you cannot rejoice
in feelings, circumstances
or conditions, rejoice
in the Lord.

– A.B. SIMPSON

GRATITUDE & ATTITUDE

UNDERSTANDING INTEGRITY
HUMUOR SUCCESS PEACEFUL WISDOM
DEDICATION HAPPINESS CONTROL INVENTIVE
IMAGINATION INTENTIONAL DISCIPLINED
PLAYFULNESS CONNECTION ENDURANCE
EQUALITY PATIENCE AWARENESS LAUGHTER

GRATITUDE & KINDNESS

gratitude jar

♡ _____
♡ _____
♡ _____
♡ _____
♡ _____
♡ _____
♡ _____
♡ _____

GRATITUDE & GROWTH

EMOTIONAL

PHYSICAL

CAREER

FAMILY

SOCIAL

RELATIONSHIPS

GOALS FOR BUILDING
A HABIT OF GRATITUDE

GOAL 1

GOAL 2

GOAL 3

GOAL 4

GOAL 5

count your
BLESSINGS

Every good and perfect gift is from above, coming down from the Father of the heavenly lights, who does not change like shifting shadows.

– JAMES 1:17, NIV

Date:

I'M GRATEFUL FOR:	HIGHLIGHT OF THE DAY:

Date:

I'M GRATEFUL FOR:	HIGHLIGHT OF THE DAY:

Date:

I'M GRATEFUL FOR:	HIGHLIGHT OF THE DAY:

Date:

I'M GRATEFUL FOR:	HIGHLIGHT OF THE DAY:

Date:

I'M GRATEFUL FOR:	HIGHLIGHT OF THE DAY:

Date:

I'M GRATEFUL FOR:	HIGHLIGHT OF THE DAY:

Date:

I'M GRATEFUL FOR:	HIGHLIGHT OF THE DAY:

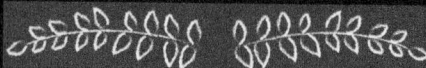

*It is not how much we have,
but how much we enjoy,
that makes happiness.*

– CHARLES SPURGEON

GRATITUDE & ATTITUDE

RESPONSIBLE
OPEN MINDEDNESS JUSTICE
AUTHENTICITY
ORIGINALITY COURAGE LOYALTY
PERSERVERANCE CONTRIBUTION
SUPPORT UNITY FUN SERVICE

GRATITUDE & KINDNESS

♡ _____
♡ _____
♡ _____
♡ _____
♡ _____
♡ _____
♡ _____
♡ _____
♡ _____
♡ _____
♡ _____

gratitude jar

♡ _____
♡ _____
♡ _____
♡ _____
♡ _____
♡ _____
♡ _____
♡ _____

GRATITUDE & GROWTH

EMOTIONAL

PHYSICAL

CAREER

FAMILY

SOCIAL

RELATIONSHIPS

GOALS FOR BUILDING A HABIT OF GRATITUDE

GOAL 1

GOAL 2

GOAL 3

GOAL 4

GOAL 5

count your
BLESSINGS

Enter into his gates with thanksgiving, and into his courts with praise: be thankful unto him, and bless his name.

– PSALM 100:4, KJV

Date:

I'M GRATEFUL FOR:	HIGHLIGHT OF THE DAY:

Date:

I'M GRATEFUL FOR:	HIGHLIGHT OF THE DAY:

Date:

I'M GRATEFUL FOR:	HIGHLIGHT OF THE DAY:

Date:

I'M GRATEFUL FOR:	HIGHLIGHT OF THE DAY:

Date:

I'M GRATEFUL FOR:	HIGHLIGHT OF THE DAY:

Date:

I'M GRATEFUL FOR:	HIGHLIGHT OF THE DAY:

Date:

I'M GRATEFUL FOR:	HIGHLIGHT OF THE DAY:

May your heart be an altar, from which the bright flame of unending thanksgiving ascends to heaven.

– MARY EUPHRASIA PELLETIER

GRATITUDE & ATTITUDE

GRATITUDE
LEARNING LEAD SENSITIVITY
ADVENTURE GROWTH PACIFIST DREAM
COMPASSION CONTENTMENT ACCEPTANCE
GENEROSITY FREEDOM INTIMACY HONESTY LISTENING HOPE DEVOTION SPONTANEOUS INTUITION
COMMUNITY DEPENDABLE WEALTH BEAUTY FAIRNESS
FRIENDLINESS

GRATITUDE & KINDNESS

♡ _____
♡ _____
♡ _____
♡ _____
♡ _____
♡ _____
♡ _____
♡ _____
♡ _____
♡ _____
♡ _____
♡ _____

gratitude jar

♡ _____
♡ _____
♡ _____
♡ _____
♡ _____
♡ _____
♡ _____
♡ _____

GRATITUDE & GROWTH

EMOTIONAL

PHYSICAL

CAREER

FAMILY

SOCIAL

RELATIONSHIPS

GOALS FOR BUILDING
A HABIT OF GRATITUDE

GOAL 1

GOAL 2

GOAL 3

GOAL 4

GOAL 5

BLESSINGS

Give thanks to the Lord and proclaim his greatness.
Let the whole world know what he has done.

– PSALM 105:1, NLT

Date:

I'M GRATEFUL FOR:	HIGHLIGHT OF THE DAY:

Date:

I'M GRATEFUL FOR:	HIGHLIGHT OF THE DAY:

Date:

I'M GRATEFUL FOR:	HIGHLIGHT OF THE DAY:

Date:

I'M GRATEFUL FOR:	HIGHLIGHT OF THE DAY:

Date:

I'M GRATEFUL FOR:	HIGHLIGHT OF THE DAY:

Date:

I'M GRATEFUL FOR:	HIGHLIGHT OF THE DAY:

Date:

I'M GRATEFUL FOR:	HIGHLIGHT OF THE DAY:

The art of being happy lies in the power of extracting happiness from common things.

– HENRY WARD BEECHER

GRATITUDE & ATTITUDE

SELF DEVELOPMENT
SELF RELIANCE
BALANCE
LOVE
CREATIVITY
NURTURING
ATTENTIVE
RELIABLE
SECURITY
POSITIVITY
FAITH
RISK TAKING
INSPIRATION
CONNECTION
HEALTH
GRACE
FAMILY
IDEALISM
RESILIENCE
ENTHUSIASM
TRUSTWORTHINESS

GRATITUDE & KINDNESS

♡ _____
♡ _____
♡ _____
♡ _____
♡ _____
♡ _____
♡ _____
♡ _____
♡ _____
♡ _____
♡ _____

gratitude jar

GRATITUDE & GROWTH

EMOTIONAL

PHYSICAL

CAREER

FAMILY

SOCIAL

RELATIONSHIPS

GOALS FOR BUILDING
A HABIT OF GRATITUDE

GOAL 1

GOAL 2

GOAL 3

GOAL 4

GOAL 5

BLESSINGS

> *I exhort therefore, that, first of all, supplications, prayers, intercessions, and giving of thanks, be made for all men.*
>
> – 1 TIMOTHY 2:1, KJV

Date:

I'M GRATEFUL FOR:	HIGHLIGHT OF THE DAY:

Date:

I'M GRATEFUL FOR:	HIGHLIGHT OF THE DAY:

Date:

I'M GRATEFUL FOR:	HIGHLIGHT OF THE DAY:

Date:

I'M GRATEFUL FOR:	HIGHLIGHT OF THE DAY:

Date:

I'M GRATEFUL FOR:	HIGHLIGHT OF THE DAY:

Date:

I'M GRATEFUL FOR:	HIGHLIGHT OF THE DAY:

Date:

I'M GRATEFUL FOR:	HIGHLIGHT OF THE DAY:

*A gift, with a
kind countenance,
is a double present.*

- THOMAS FULLER

GRATITUDE & ATTITUDE

HAPPINESS SUCCESS
HUMUOR
UNDERSTANDING INTEGRITY
DEDICATION
IMAGINATION
PLAYFULNESS
INTENTIONAL
EQUALITY
CONNECTION
PATIENCE AWARENESS
PEACEFUL
CONTROL
DISCIPLINED
WISDOM
INVENTIVE
ENDURANCE
LAUGHTER

GRATITUDE & KINDNESS

♡ _____
♡ _____
♡ _____
♡ _____
♡ _____
♡ _____
♡ _____
♡ _____
♡ _____
♡ _____
♡ _____

gratitude jar

♡ _____
♡ _____
♡ _____
♡ _____
♡ _____
♡ _____
♡ _____
♡ _____

GRATITUDE & GROWTH

EMOTIONAL

PHYSICAL

CAREER

FAMILY

SOCIAL

RELATIONSHIPS

GOALS FOR BUILDING
A HABIT OF GRATITUDE

GOAL 1

GOAL 2

GOAL 3

GOAL 4

GOAL 5

count your

BLESSINGS

Let the word of Christ richly dwell within you, with all wisdom Teaching and admonishing one another with psalms and hymns and spiritual songs, singing with thankfulness in your hearts to God.

– COLOSSIANS 3:16, NASB

Date:

I'M GRATEFUL FOR:	HIGHLIGHT OF THE DAY:

Date:

I'M GRATEFUL FOR:	HIGHLIGHT OF THE DAY:

Date:

I'M GRATEFUL FOR:	HIGHLIGHT OF THE DAY:

Date:

I'M GRATEFUL FOR:	HIGHLIGHT OF THE DAY:

Date:

I'M GRATEFUL FOR:	HIGHLIGHT OF THE DAY:

Date:

I'M GRATEFUL FOR:	HIGHLIGHT OF THE DAY:

Date:

I'M GRATEFUL FOR:	HIGHLIGHT OF THE DAY:

To be always in a thankful state of heart before God is not to be considered a high plane of spirituality but rather the normal attitude of one who believes that "all things work together for good to them that love God, who are called according to his purpose."

– WILLIAM LAW

GRATITUDE & ATTITUDE

RESPONSIBLE
OPEN MINDEDNESS JUSTICE
AUTHENTICITY
ORIGINALITY
PERSERVERANCE
COURAGE LOYALTY
CONTRIBUTION
SUPPORT UNITY FUN SERVICE

GRATITUDE & KINDNESS

gratitude jar

♡ _____
♡ _____
♡ _____
♡ _____
♡ _____
♡ _____
♡ _____
♡ _____

GRATITUDE & GROWTH

EMOTIONAL

PHYSICAL

CAREER

FAMILY

SOCIAL

RELATIONSHIPS

GOALS FOR BUILDING
A HABIT OF GRATITUDE

GOAL 1

GOAL 2

GOAL 3

GOAL 4

GOAL 5

count your
BLESSINGS

The righteous will rejoice in the Lord and take refuge in him; all the upright in heart will glory in him!

– PSALM 64:10, NIV

Date:

I'M GRATEFUL FOR:	HIGHLIGHT OF THE DAY:

Date:

I'M GRATEFUL FOR:	HIGHLIGHT OF THE DAY:

Date:

I'M GRATEFUL FOR:	HIGHLIGHT OF THE DAY:

Date:

I'M GRATEFUL FOR:	HIGHLIGHT OF THE DAY:

Date:

I'M GRATEFUL FOR:	HIGHLIGHT OF THE DAY:

Date:

I'M GRATEFUL FOR:	HIGHLIGHT OF THE DAY:

Date:

I'M GRATEFUL FOR:	HIGHLIGHT OF THE DAY:

Prayer is the soul's breathing itself into the bosom of its heavenly Father.

– THOMAS WATSON

GRATITUDE & ATTITUDE

GRATITUDE
LEARNING LEAD SENSITIVITY
ADVENTURE CONTENTMENT ACCEPTANCE GROWTH PACIFIST DREAM SPONTANEOUS INTUITION
COMPASSION
GENEROSITY FREEDOM INTIMACY HONESTY LISTENING HOPE DEVOTION
COMMUNITY DEPENDABLE WEALTH CONTENTMENT BEAUTY FAIRNESS
FRIENDLINESS

GRATITUDE & KINDNESS

♡ _____
♡ _____
♡ _____
♡ _____
♡ _____
♡ _____
♡ _____
♡ _____
♡ _____
♡ _____
♡ _____

gratitude jar

♡ _____
♡ _____
♡ _____
♡ _____
♡ _____
♡ _____
♡ _____
♡ _____

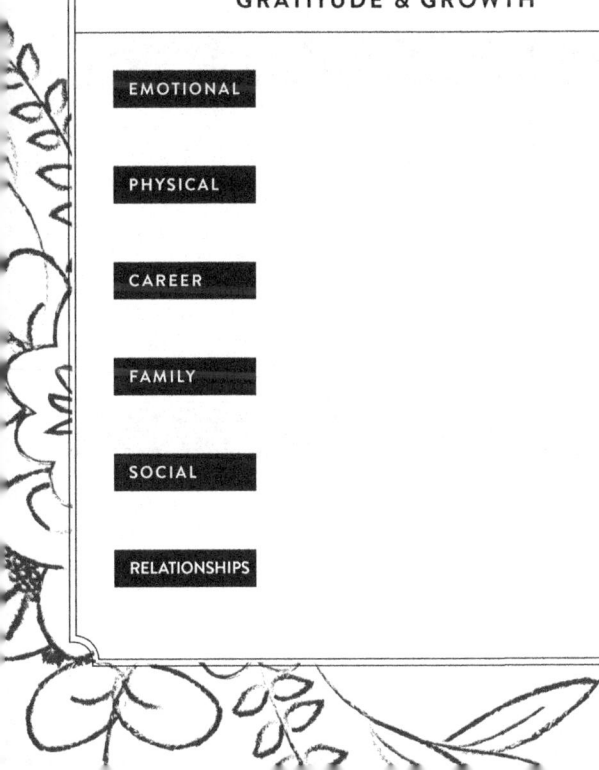

GRATITUDE & GROWTH

EMOTIONAL

PHYSICAL

CAREER

FAMILY

SOCIAL

RELATIONSHIPS

GOALS FOR BUILDING
A HABIT OF GRATITUDE

GOAL 1

GOAL 2

GOAL 3

GOAL 4

GOAL 5

count your
BLESSINGS

And my God will supply all your needs according to His riches in glory in Christ Jesus.

— PHILIPPIANS 4:19, NASB

Date:

I'M GRATEFUL FOR:	HIGHLIGHT OF THE DAY:

Date:

I'M GRATEFUL FOR:	HIGHLIGHT OF THE DAY:

Date:

I'M GRATEFUL FOR:	HIGHLIGHT OF THE DAY:

Date:

I'M GRATEFUL FOR:	HIGHLIGHT OF THE DAY:

Date:

I'M GRATEFUL FOR:	HIGHLIGHT OF THE DAY:

Date:

I'M GRATEFUL FOR:	HIGHLIGHT OF THE DAY:

Date:

I'M GRATEFUL FOR:	HIGHLIGHT OF THE DAY:

Man should not consider his material possession his own, but as common to all, so as to share them without hesitation when others are in need.

– THOMAS AQUINAS

GRATITUDE & ATTITUDE

SELF DEVELOPMENT
SELF RELIANCE
BALANCE
ATTENTIVE
CREATIVITY
LOVE
IDEALISM
NURTURING RESILIENCE
RELIABLE
SECURITY
POSITIVITY
HEALTH
GRACE
FAMILY
FAITH
RISK TAKING
ENTHUSIASM
NURTURING
INSPIRATION
CONNECTION
TRUSTWORTHINESS

GRATITUDE & KINDNESS

♡ _____
♡ _____
♡ _____
♡ _____
♡ _____
♡ _____
♡ _____
♡ _____
♡ _____
♡ _____
♡ _____

gratitude jar

♡ _____
♡ _____
♡ _____
♡ _____
♡ _____
♡ _____
♡ _____
♡ _____

GRATITUDE & GROWTH

EMOTIONAL

PHYSICAL

CAREER

FAMILY

SOCIAL

RELATIONSHIPS

GOALS FOR BUILDING A HABIT OF GRATITUDE

GOAL 1

GOAL 2

GOAL 3

GOAL 4

GOAL 5

count your
BLESSINGS

Surely your goodness and love will follow me all the days of my life, and I will dwell in the house of the Lord forever.

– PSALM 23:6, NIV

Date:

I'M GRATEFUL FOR:	HIGHLIGHT OF THE DAY:

Date:

I'M GRATEFUL FOR:	HIGHLIGHT OF THE DAY:

Date:

I'M GRATEFUL FOR:	HIGHLIGHT OF THE DAY:

Date:

I'M GRATEFUL FOR:	HIGHLIGHT OF THE DAY:

Date:

I'M GRATEFUL FOR:	HIGHLIGHT OF THE DAY:

Date:

I'M GRATEFUL FOR:	HIGHLIGHT OF THE DAY:

Date:

I'M GRATEFUL FOR:	HIGHLIGHT OF THE DAY:

I know of no better thermometer to your spiritual temperature than this, the measure of the intensity of your prayer.

– CHARLES SPURGEON

GRATITUDE & ATTITUDE

IMAGINATION
DEDICATION HAPPINESS SUCCESS
UNDERSTANDING INTEGRITY
HUMUOR PEACEFUL WISDOM
CONTROL
PLAYFULNESS INTENTIONAL
DISCIPLINED INVENTIVE
EQUALITY CONNECTION ENDURANCE
PATIENCE AWARENESS LAUGHTER

GRATITUDE & KINDNESS

♡ _____
♡ _____
♡ _____
♡ _____
♡ _____
♡ _____
♡ _____
♡ _____
♡ _____
♡ _____
♡ _____

gratitude jar

♥ _____
♥ _____
♥ _____
♥ _____
♥ _____
♥ _____
♥ _____
♥ _____

GRATITUDE & GROWTH

EMOTIONAL

PHYSICAL

CAREER

FAMILY

SOCIAL

RELATIONSHIPS

GOALS FOR BUILDING A HABIT OF GRATITUDE

GOAL 1

GOAL 2

GOAL 3

GOAL 4

GOAL 5

count your
BLESSINGS

> *And whatsoever we ask, we receive of him, because we keep his commandments, and do those things that are pleasing in his sight.*
>
> – 1 JOHN 3:22, KJV

Date:

I'M GRATEFUL FOR:	HIGHLIGHT OF THE DAY:

Date:

I'M GRATEFUL FOR:	HIGHLIGHT OF THE DAY:

Date:

I'M GRATEFUL FOR:	HIGHLIGHT OF THE DAY:

Date:

I'M GRATEFUL FOR:	HIGHLIGHT OF THE DAY:

Date:

I'M GRATEFUL FOR:	HIGHLIGHT OF THE DAY:

Date:

I'M GRATEFUL FOR:	HIGHLIGHT OF THE DAY:

Date:

I'M GRATEFUL FOR:	HIGHLIGHT OF THE DAY:

What does love look like? It has the hands to help others. It has the feet to hasten to the poor and needy. It has eyes to see misery and want. It has the ears to hear the sighs and sorrows of men. That is what love looks like.

– AUGUSTINE

GRATITUDE & ATTITUDE

RESPONSIBLE
OPEN MINDEDNESS JUSTICE
AUTHENTICITY
ORIGINALITY
PERSERVERANCE
COURAGE LOYALTY
CONTRIBUTION
SUPPORT UNITY FUN SERVICE

GRATITUDE & KINDNESS

♡ _____
♡ _____
♡ _____
♡ _____
♡ _____
♡ _____
♡ _____
♡ _____
♡ _____
♡ _____
♡ _____

gratitude jar

♡ _____
♡ _____
♡ _____
♡ _____
♡ _____
♡ _____
♡ _____
♡ _____

GRATITUDE & GROWTH

EMOTIONAL

PHYSICAL

CAREER

FAMILY

SOCIAL

RELATIONSHIPS

GOALS FOR BUILDING
A HABIT OF GRATITUDE

GOAL 1

GOAL 2

GOAL 3

GOAL 4

GOAL 5

count your
BLESSINGS

Therefore, my beloved brethren, be steadfast, immovable, always abounding in the work of the Lord, knowing that your toil is not in vain in the Lord.

— 1 CORINTHIANS 15:58, NASB

Date:

I'M GRATEFUL FOR:	HIGHLIGHT OF THE DAY:

Date:

I'M GRATEFUL FOR:	HIGHLIGHT OF THE DAY:

Date:

I'M GRATEFUL FOR:	HIGHLIGHT OF THE DAY:

Date:

I'M GRATEFUL FOR:	HIGHLIGHT OF THE DAY:

Date:

I'M GRATEFUL FOR:	HIGHLIGHT OF THE DAY:

Date:

I'M GRATEFUL FOR:	HIGHLIGHT OF THE DAY:

Date:

I'M GRATEFUL FOR:	HIGHLIGHT OF THE DAY:

it melts His heart; and opens His hand. God cannot deny a praying soul.

– THOMAS WATSON

GRATITUDE & ATTITUDE

GRATITUDE
LEARNING LEAD SENSITIVITY
ADVENTURE CONTENTMENT ACCEPTANCE GROWTH PACIFIST DREAM
COMPASSION SPONTANEOUS INTUITION
GENEROSITY INTIMACY HONESTY LISTENING HOPE DEVOTION
FREEDOM COMMUNITY DEPENDABLE WEALTH BEAUTY FAIRNESS
FRIENDLINESS

GRATITUDE & KINDNESS

♡ _____
♡ _____
♡ _____
♡ _____
♡ _____
♡ _____
♡ _____
♡ _____
♡ _____
♡ _____
♡ _____

gratitude jar

♡ _____
♡ _____
♡ _____
♡ _____
♡ _____
♡ _____
♡ _____
♡ _____

GRATITUDE & GROWTH

EMOTIONAL

PHYSICAL

CAREER

FAMILY

SOCIAL

RELATIONSHIPS

GOALS FOR BUILDING
A HABIT OF GRATITUDE

GOAL 1

GOAL 2

GOAL 3

GOAL 4

GOAL 5

count your
BLESSINGS

Through Jesus, therefore, let us continually offer to God a sacrifice of praise-the fruit of lips that openly profess his name.

— HEBREWS 13:15, NIV

Date:

I'M GRATEFUL FOR:	HIGHLIGHT OF THE DAY:

Date:

I'M GRATEFUL FOR:	HIGHLIGHT OF THE DAY:

Date:

I'M GRATEFUL FOR:	HIGHLIGHT OF THE DAY:

Date:

I'M GRATEFUL FOR:	HIGHLIGHT OF THE DAY:

Date:

I'M GRATEFUL FOR:	HIGHLIGHT OF THE DAY:

Date:

I'M GRATEFUL FOR:	HIGHLIGHT OF THE DAY:

Date:

I'M GRATEFUL FOR:	HIGHLIGHT OF THE DAY:

What we count the ills of life are often blessings in disguise, resulting in good to us in the end. Though for the present not joyous but grievous, yet, if received in a right spirit, they work out fruits of righteousness for us at last.

– MATTHEW HENRY

GRATITUDE & ATTITUDE

SELF DEVELOPMENT
SELF RELIANCE
BALANCE
CREATIVITY
NURTURING
ATTENTIVE
LOVE
IDEALISM
RELIABLE
SECURITY
POSITIVITY
HEALTH
GRACE
FAMILY
NURTURING
RESILIENCE
FAITH
RISK TAKING
ENTHUSIASM
INSPIRATION
CONNECTION
TRUSTWORTHINESS

GRATITUDE & KINDNESS

♡ _____
♡ _____
♡ _____
♡ _____
♡ _____
♡ _____
♡ _____
♡ _____
♡ _____
♡ _____
♡ _____

gratitude jar

♡ _____
♡ _____
♡ _____
♡ _____
♡ _____
♡ _____
♡ _____
♡ _____

GRATITUDE & GROWTH

EMOTIONAL

PHYSICAL

CAREER

FAMILY

SOCIAL

RELATIONSHIPS

GOALS FOR BUILDING
A HABIT OF GRATITUDE

GOAL 1

GOAL 2

GOAL 3

GOAL 4

GOAL 5

count your
BLESSINGS

But those who trust in the Lord will find new strength.
They will soar high on wings like eagles. They will run
and not grow weary. They will walk and not faint.

– ISAIAH 40:31, NLT

Date:

I'M GRATEFUL FOR:	HIGHLIGHT OF THE DAY:

Date:

I'M GRATEFUL FOR:	HIGHLIGHT OF THE DAY:

Date:

I'M GRATEFUL FOR:	HIGHLIGHT OF THE DAY:

Date:

I'M GRATEFUL FOR:	HIGHLIGHT OF THE DAY:

Date:

I'M GRATEFUL FOR:	HIGHLIGHT OF THE DAY:

Date:

I'M GRATEFUL FOR:	HIGHLIGHT OF THE DAY:

Date:

I'M GRATEFUL FOR:	HIGHLIGHT OF THE DAY:

The private and personal blessings we enjoy - the blessings of immunity, safeguard, liberty and integrity - deserve the thanksgiving of a whole life.

— JEREMY TAYLOR

GRATITUDE & ATTITUDE

UNDERSTANDING INTEGRITY
HUMUOR SUCCESS PEACEFUL CONTROL WISDOM
DEDICATION HAPPINESS
IMAGINATION PLAYFULNESS INTENTIONAL DISCIPLINED INVENTIVE
CONNECTION ENDURANCE LAUGHTER
EQUALITY PATIENCE AWARENESS

GRATITUDE & KINDNESS

gratitude jar

♡ _____
♡ _____
♡ _____
♡ _____
♡ _____
♡ _____
♡ _____
♡ _____
_____

GRATITUDE & GROWTH

EMOTIONAL

PHYSICAL

CAREER

FAMILY

SOCIAL

RELATIONSHIPS

GOALS FOR BUILDING A HABIT OF GRATITUDE

GOAL 1

GOAL 2

GOAL 3

GOAL 4

GOAL 5

count your
BLESSINGS

The Lord has done great things for us, and we are filled with joy.

– PSALM 126:3, NIV

Date:

I'M GRATEFUL FOR:	HIGHLIGHT OF THE DAY:

Date:

I'M GRATEFUL FOR:	HIGHLIGHT OF THE DAY:

Date:

I'M GRATEFUL FOR:	HIGHLIGHT OF THE DAY:

Date:

I'M GRATEFUL FOR:	HIGHLIGHT OF THE DAY:

Date:

I'M GRATEFUL FOR:	HIGHLIGHT OF THE DAY:

Date:

I'M GRATEFUL FOR:	HIGHLIGHT OF THE DAY:

Date:

I'M GRATEFUL FOR:	HIGHLIGHT OF THE DAY:

The soul that gives thanks can find comfort in everything; The soul that complains can find comfort in nothing.

– HANNAH WHITALL SMITH

GRATITUDE & ATTITUDE

RESPONSIBLE
OPEN MINDEDNESS JUSTICE
AUTHENTICITY
ORIGINALITY
PERSERVERANCE
COURAGE LOYALTY
CONTRIBUTION
SUPPORT UNITY FUN SERVICE

GRATITUDE & KINDNESS

♡ _____
♡ _____
♡ _____
♡ _____
♡ _____
♡ _____
♡ _____
♡ _____
♡ _____
♡ _____
♡ _____

gratitude jar

♡ _____
♡ _____
♡ _____
♡ _____
♡ _____
♡ _____
♡ _____
♡ _____

GRATITUDE & GROWTH

EMOTIONAL

PHYSICAL

CAREER

FAMILY

SOCIAL

RELATIONSHIPS

GOALS FOR BUILDING A HABIT OF GRATITUDE

GOAL 1

GOAL 2

GOAL 3

GOAL 4

GOAL 5

count your
BLESSINGS

Let us come before his presence with thanksgiving, and make a joyful noise unto him with psalms. For the Lord is a great God, and a great King above all gods.

– PSALM 95:2-3, KJV

Date:

I'M GRATEFUL FOR:	HIGHLIGHT OF THE DAY:

Date:

I'M GRATEFUL FOR:	HIGHLIGHT OF THE DAY:

Date:

I'M GRATEFUL FOR:	HIGHLIGHT OF THE DAY:

Date:

I'M GRATEFUL FOR:	HIGHLIGHT OF THE DAY:

Date:

I'M GRATEFUL FOR:	HIGHLIGHT OF THE DAY:

Date:

I'M GRATEFUL FOR:	HIGHLIGHT OF THE DAY:

Date:

I'M GRATEFUL FOR:	HIGHLIGHT OF THE DAY:

God will either give you what you ask, or something far better.

– ROBERT MURRAY MCCHEYNE

GRATITUDE & ATTITUDE

LEARNING LEAD SENSITIVITY GRATITUDE
ADVENTURE CONTENTMENT GROWTH PACIFIST DREAM
COMPASSION ACCEPTANCE SPONTANEOUS INTUITION
GENEROSITY INTIMACY HOPE DEVOTION
FREEDOM HONESTY LISTENING
COMMUNITY CONTENTMENT BEAUTY FAIRNESS
DEPENDABLE WEALTH ACCEPTANCE
FRIENDLINESS

GRATITUDE & KINDNESS

♡ _____
♡ _____
♡ _____
♡ _____
♡ _____
♡ _____
♡ _____
♡ _____
♡ _____
♡ _____
♡ _____

gratitude jar

♡ _____
♡ _____
♡ _____
♡ _____
♡ _____
♡ _____
♡ _____
♡ _____

GRATITUDE & GROWTH

- EMOTIONAL
- PHYSICAL
- CAREER
- FAMILY
- SOCIAL
- RELATIONSHIPS

GOALS FOR BUILDING A HABIT OF GRATITUDE

- GOAL 1
- GOAL 2
- GOAL 3
- GOAL 4
- GOAL 5

count your
BLESSINGS

The Lord is my strength and my shield; my heart trusts in him, and he helps me. My heart leaps for joy, and with my song I praise him.

– PSALM 28:7, NIV

Date:

I'M GRATEFUL FOR:	HIGHLIGHT OF THE DAY:

Date:

I'M GRATEFUL FOR:	HIGHLIGHT OF THE DAY:

Date:

I'M GRATEFUL FOR:	HIGHLIGHT OF THE DAY:

Date:

I'M GRATEFUL FOR:	HIGHLIGHT OF THE DAY:

Date:

I'M GRATEFUL FOR:	HIGHLIGHT OF THE DAY:

Date:

I'M GRATEFUL FOR:	HIGHLIGHT OF THE DAY:

Date:

I'M GRATEFUL FOR:	HIGHLIGHT OF THE DAY:

Thou who hast given so much to me, give me one more thing: a grateful heart!

– GEORGE HERBERT

GRATITUDE & ATTITUDE

SELF DEVELOPMENT
SELF RELIANCE
BALANCE
LOVE
CREATIVITY
NURTURING
ATTENTIVE
RELIABLE
SECURITY
POSITIVITY
HEALTH
GRACE
FAMILY
IDEALISM
NURTURING RESILIENCE
FAITH
RISK TAKING
ENTHUSIASM
CONNECTION
INSPIRATION
TRUSTWORTHINESS

GRATITUDE & KINDNESS

gratitude jar

♡ _____
♡ _____
♡ _____
♡ _____
♡ _____
♡ _____
♡ _____
♡ _____

GRATITUDE & GROWTH

EMOTIONAL

PHYSICAL

CAREER

FAMILY

SOCIAL

RELATIONSHIPS

GOALS FOR BUILDING A HABIT OF GRATITUDE

GOAL 1

GOAL 2

GOAL 3

GOAL 4

GOAL 5

count your
BLESSINGS

It is a good thing to give thanks unto the Lord, and to sing praises unto thy name, O Most High.

– PSALM 92:1, KJV

Date:

I'M GRATEFUL FOR:	HIGHLIGHT OF THE DAY:

Date:

I'M GRATEFUL FOR:	HIGHLIGHT OF THE DAY:

Date:

I'M GRATEFUL FOR:	HIGHLIGHT OF THE DAY:

Date:

I'M GRATEFUL FOR:	HIGHLIGHT OF THE DAY:

Date:

I'M GRATEFUL FOR:	HIGHLIGHT OF THE DAY:

Date:

I'M GRATEFUL FOR:	HIGHLIGHT OF THE DAY:

Date:

I'M GRATEFUL FOR:	HIGHLIGHT OF THE DAY:

It is His joy that remains in us that makes our joy full.

– A.B. SIMPSON

GRATITUDE & ATTITUDE

IMAGINATION DEDICATION HAPPINESS HUMUOR UNDERSTANDING INTEGRITY SUCCESS PEACEFUL CONTROL WISDOM INVENTIVE DISCIPLINED PLAYFULNESS INTENTIONAL EQUALITY CONNECTION ENDURANCE LAUGHTER PATIENCE AWARENESS

GRATITUDE & KINDNESS

gratitude jar

♥ _____
♥ _____
♥ _____
♥ _____
♥ _____
♥ _____
♥ _____
♥ _____

GRATITUDE & GROWTH

EMOTIONAL

PHYSICAL

CAREER

FAMILY

SOCIAL

RELATIONSHIPS

GOALS FOR BUILDING A HABIT OF GRATITUDE

GOAL 1

GOAL 2

GOAL 3

GOAL 4

GOAL 5

count your
BLESSINGS

Let all that I am praise the Lord; may I never forget the good things he does for me.

– PSALM 103:2, NLT

Date:

I'M GRATEFUL FOR:	HIGHLIGHT OF THE DAY:

Date:

I'M GRATEFUL FOR:	HIGHLIGHT OF THE DAY:

Date:

I'M GRATEFUL FOR:	HIGHLIGHT OF THE DAY:

Date:

I'M GRATEFUL FOR:	HIGHLIGHT OF THE DAY:

Date:

I'M GRATEFUL FOR:	HIGHLIGHT OF THE DAY:

Date:

I'M GRATEFUL FOR:	HIGHLIGHT OF THE DAY:

Date:

I'M GRATEFUL FOR:	HIGHLIGHT OF THE DAY:

Happiness is the natural flower of duty.

– PHILLIPS BROOKS

GRATITUDE & ATTITUDE

RESPONSIBLE
OPEN MINDEDNESS JUSTICE
AUTHENTICITY
ORIGINALITY
PERSERVERANCE
COURAGE LOYALTY
CONTRIBUTION
SUPPORT UNITY FUN SERVICE

GRATITUDE & KINDNESS

♡ _____
♡ _____
♡ _____
♡ _____
♡ _____
♡ _____
♡ _____
♡ _____
♡ _____
♡ _____
♡ _____

gratitude jar

- ♡ _____
- ♡ _____
- ♡ _____
- ♡ _____
- ♡ _____
- ♡ _____
- ♡ _____
- ♡ _____

GRATITUDE & GROWTH

- **EMOTIONAL**
- **PHYSICAL**
- **CAREER**
- **FAMILY**
- **SOCIAL**
- **RELATIONSHIPS**

GOALS FOR BUILDING A HABIT OF GRATITUDE

- **GOAL 1**
- **GOAL 2**
- **GOAL 3**
- **GOAL 4**
- **GOAL 5**

count your
BLESSINGS

*I will praise the name of God with a song,
and will magnify him with thanksgiving.*

– PSALM 69:30, KJV

Date:

I'M GRATEFUL FOR:	HIGHLIGHT OF THE DAY:

Date:

I'M GRATEFUL FOR:	HIGHLIGHT OF THE DAY:

Date:

I'M GRATEFUL FOR:	HIGHLIGHT OF THE DAY:

Date:

I'M GRATEFUL FOR:	HIGHLIGHT OF THE DAY:

Date:

I'M GRATEFUL FOR:	HIGHLIGHT OF THE DAY:

Date:

I'M GRATEFUL FOR:	HIGHLIGHT OF THE DAY:

Date:

I'M GRATEFUL FOR:	HIGHLIGHT OF THE DAY:

Giving is true having.

— CHARLES SPURGEON

GRATITUDE & KINDNESS

GRATITUDE
LEARNING LEAD SENSITIVITY GROWTH PACIFIST DREAM
ADVENTURE CONTENTMENT ACCEPTANCE SPONTANEOUS INTUITION
COMPASSION INTIMACY HONESTY HOPE DEVOTION
GENEROSITY FREEDOM LISTENING BEAUTY FAIRNESS
COMMUNITY DEPENDABLE WEALTH FRIENDLINESS

gratitude jar

♡ _____
♡ _____
♡ _____
♡ _____
♡ _____
♡ _____
♡ _____
♡ _____

GRATITUDE & GROWTH

EMOTIONAL

PHYSICAL

CAREER

FAMILY

SOCIAL

RELATIONSHIPS

GOALS FOR BUILDING A HABIT OF GRATITUDE

GOAL 1

GOAL 2

GOAL 3

GOAL 4

GOAL 5

count your
BLESSINGS

Enter His gates with thanksgiving and His courts with praise. Give thanks to Him, bless His name. For the Lord is good; His lovingkindness is everlasting and His faithfulness to all generations

– PSALM 100:4-5, NASB

Date:

I'M GRATEFUL FOR:	HIGHLIGHT OF THE DAY:

Date:

I'M GRATEFUL FOR:	HIGHLIGHT OF THE DAY:

Date:

I'M GRATEFUL FOR:	HIGHLIGHT OF THE DAY:

Date:

I'M GRATEFUL FOR:	HIGHLIGHT OF THE DAY:

Date:

I'M GRATEFUL FOR:	HIGHLIGHT OF THE DAY:

Date:

I'M GRATEFUL FOR:	HIGHLIGHT OF THE DAY:

Date:

I'M GRATEFUL FOR:	HIGHLIGHT OF THE DAY:

> He is your friend who pushes you nearer to God.

— ABRAHAM KUYPER

GRATITUDE & ATTITUDE

SELF DEVELOPMENT
SELF RELIANCE
BALANCE
ATTENTIVE
LOVE CREATIVITY NURTURING RELIABLE SECURITY
POSITIVITY
HEALTH GRACE FAMILY IDEALISM FAITH RISK TAKING ENTHUSIASM
NURTURING RESILIENCE
INSPIRATION CONNECTION
TRUSTWORTHINESS

GRATITUDE & KINDNESS

♡ _____
♡ _____
♡ _____
♡ _____
♡ _____
♡ _____
♡ _____
♡ _____
♡ _____
♡ _____
♡ _____

gratitude jar

♡ _____
♡ _____
♡ _____
♡ _____
♡ _____
♡ _____
♡ _____
♡ _____

GRATITUDE & GROWTH

EMOTIONAL

PHYSICAL

CAREER

FAMILY

SOCIAL

RELATIONSHIPS

GOALS FOR BUILDING
A HABIT OF GRATITUDE

GOAL 1

GOAL 2

GOAL 3

GOAL 4

GOAL 5

count your

BLESSINGS

> "Amen! Praise and glory and wisdom and thanks and honor and power and strength be to our God for ever and ever. Amen!"
>
> – REVELATION 7:12, NIV

Date:

I'M GRATEFUL FOR:	HIGHLIGHT OF THE DAY:

Date:

I'M GRATEFUL FOR:	HIGHLIGHT OF THE DAY:

Date:

I'M GRATEFUL FOR:	HIGHLIGHT OF THE DAY:

Date:

I'M GRATEFUL FOR:	HIGHLIGHT OF THE DAY:

Date:

I'M GRATEFUL FOR:	HIGHLIGHT OF THE DAY:

Date:

I'M GRATEFUL FOR:	HIGHLIGHT OF THE DAY:

Date:

I'M GRATEFUL FOR:	HIGHLIGHT OF THE DAY:

Our prayers run along one road and God's answers by another, and by and by they meet.

– ADONIRAM JUDSON

GRATITUDE & ATTITUDE

UNDERSTANDING INTEGRITY
HUMUOR PEACEFUL CONTROL WISDOM
DEDICATION HAPPINESS SUCCESS
IMAGINATION INTENTIONAL DISCIPLINED INVENTIVE
PLAYFULNESS
EQUALITY CONNECTION ENDURANCE
PATIENCE AWARENESS LAUGHTER

GRATITUDE & KINDNESS

gratitude jar

♡ _____
♡ _____
♡ _____
♡ _____
♡ _____
♡ _____
♡ _____
♡ _____

GRATITUDE & GROWTH

EMOTIONAL

PHYSICAL

CAREER

FAMILY

SOCIAL

RELATIONSHIPS

GOALS FOR BUILDING A HABIT OF GRATITUDE

GOAL 1

GOAL 2

GOAL 3

GOAL 4

GOAL 5

count your
BLESSINGS

Offer unto God thanksgiving; and pay thy vows unto the most High.

– PSALM 50:14, KJV

Date:

I'M GRATEFUL FOR:	HIGHLIGHT OF THE DAY:

Date:

I'M GRATEFUL FOR:	HIGHLIGHT OF THE DAY:

Date:

I'M GRATEFUL FOR:	HIGHLIGHT OF THE DAY:

Date:

I'M GRATEFUL FOR:	HIGHLIGHT OF THE DAY:

Date:

I'M GRATEFUL FOR:	HIGHLIGHT OF THE DAY:

Date:

I'M GRATEFUL FOR:	HIGHLIGHT OF THE DAY:

Date:

I'M GRATEFUL FOR:	HIGHLIGHT OF THE DAY:

Faith without thankfulness lacks strength and fortitude.

– JOHN HENRY JOWETT

GRATITUDE & ATTITUDE

RESPONSIBLE
OPEN MINDEDNESS JUSTICE
AUTHENTICITY
ORIGINALITY
PERSERVERANCE
COURAGE LOYALTY CONTRIBUTION
SUPPORT UNITY FUN SERVICE

GRATITUDE & KINDNESS

gratitude jar

♡ _____
♡ _____
♡ _____
♡ _____
♡ _____
♡ _____
♡ _____
♡ _____

GRATITUDE & GROWTH

EMOTIONAL

PHYSICAL

CAREER

FAMILY

SOCIAL

RELATIONSHIPS

GOALS FOR BUILDING A HABIT OF GRATITUDE

GOAL 1

GOAL 2

GOAL 3

GOAL 4

GOAL 5

count your
BLESSINGS

Praise be to the God and Father of our Lord Jesus Christ, who has blessed us in the heavenly realms with every spiritual blessing in Christ.

– EPHESIANS 1:3, NIV

Date:

I'M GRATEFUL FOR:	HIGHLIGHT OF THE DAY:

Date:

I'M GRATEFUL FOR:	HIGHLIGHT OF THE DAY:

Date:

I'M GRATEFUL FOR:	HIGHLIGHT OF THE DAY:

Date:

I'M GRATEFUL FOR:	HIGHLIGHT OF THE DAY:

Date:

I'M GRATEFUL FOR:	HIGHLIGHT OF THE DAY:

Date:

I'M GRATEFUL FOR:	HIGHLIGHT OF THE DAY:

Date:

I'M GRATEFUL FOR:	HIGHLIGHT OF THE DAY:

Oh, what great happiness and bliss, what exaltation it is to address oneself to the Eternal Father. Always, without fail, value this joy which has been accorded to you by God's infinite grace.

– JOHN OF KRONSTADT

GRATITUDE & ATTITUDE

GRATITUDE
LEAD SENSITIVITY
LEARNING GROWTH PACIFIST
ADVENTURE ACCEPTANCE DREAM SPONTANEOUS INTUITION
COMPASSION CONTENTMENT
GENEROSITY INTIMACY HONESTY HOPE DEVOTION
FREEDOM LISTENING
COMMUNITY WEALTH ACCEPTANCE BEAUTY FAIRNESS
DEPENDABLE FRIENDLINESS

GRATITUDE & KINDNESS

- ♡ _____
- ♡ _____
- ♡ _____
- ♡ _____
- ♡ _____
- ♡ _____
- ♡ _____
- ♡ _____
- ♡ _____
- ♡ _____
- ♡ _____

gratitude jar

♡ _____
♡ _____
♡ _____
♡ _____
♡ _____
♡ _____
♡ _____
♡ _____

GRATITUDE & GROWTH

EMOTIONAL

PHYSICAL

CAREER

FAMILY

SOCIAL

RELATIONSHIPS

GOALS FOR BUILDING
A HABIT OF GRATITUDE

GOAL 1

GOAL 2

GOAL 3

GOAL 4

GOAL 5

count your
BLESSINGS

I will give thanks to you, Lord, with all my heart;
I will tell of all your wonderful deeds.

– PSALM 9:1, NIV

Date:

I'M GRATEFUL FOR:	HIGHLIGHT OF THE DAY:

Date:

I'M GRATEFUL FOR:	HIGHLIGHT OF THE DAY:

Date:

I'M GRATEFUL FOR:	HIGHLIGHT OF THE DAY:

Date:

I'M GRATEFUL FOR:	HIGHLIGHT OF THE DAY:

Date:

I'M GRATEFUL FOR:	HIGHLIGHT OF THE DAY:

Date:

I'M GRATEFUL FOR:	HIGHLIGHT OF THE DAY:

Date:

I'M GRATEFUL FOR:	HIGHLIGHT OF THE DAY:

Old friends are best. King James used to call for his old shoes; they were the easiest for his feet.

– JOHN SELDEN

GRATITUDE & ATTITUDE

SELF DEVELOPMENT
SELF RELIANCE
BALANCE
ATTENTIVE
LOVE
RELIABLE SECURITY
CREATIVITY NURTURING POSITIVITY
HEALTH GRACE FAMILY IDEALISM NURTURING RESILIENCE FAITH RISK TAKING ENTHUSIASM
INSPIRATION CONNECTION
TRUSTWORTHINESS

GRATITUDE & KINDNESS

gratitude jar

- ♡ _____
- ♡ _____
- ♡ _____
- ♡ _____
- ♡ _____
- ♡ _____
- ♡ _____
- ♡ _____

GRATITUDE & GROWTH

- EMOTIONAL
- PHYSICAL
- CAREER
- FAMILY
- SOCIAL
- RELATIONSHIPS

GOALS FOR BUILDING A HABIT OF GRATITUDE

- GOAL 1
- GOAL 2
- GOAL 3
- GOAL 4
- GOAL 5

count your
BLESSINGS

Always be joyful. Never stop praying. Be thankful in all circumstances, for this is God's will for you who belong to Christ Jesus.

– 1 THESSALONIANS 5:16-18, NLT

Date:

I'M GRATEFUL FOR:		HIGHLIGHT OF THE DAY:

Date:

I'M GRATEFUL FOR:		HIGHLIGHT OF THE DAY:

Date:

I'M GRATEFUL FOR:		HIGHLIGHT OF THE DAY:

Date:

I'M GRATEFUL FOR:	HIGHLIGHT OF THE DAY:

Date:

I'M GRATEFUL FOR:	HIGHLIGHT OF THE DAY:

Date:

I'M GRATEFUL FOR:	HIGHLIGHT OF THE DAY:

Date:

I'M GRATEFUL FOR:	HIGHLIGHT OF THE DAY:

Prayer is not only asking, it is an attitude of heart that produces an atmosphere in which asking is perfectly natural, and Jesus says, "every one that asketh receiveth."

– OSWALD CHAMBERS

GRATITUDE & ATTITUDE

GRATITUDE & KINDNESS

gratitude jar

- ♡ _____
- ♡ _____
- ♡ _____
- ♡ _____
- ♡ _____
- ♡ _____
- ♡ _____
- ♡ _____

GRATITUDE & GROWTH

- EMOTIONAL
- PHYSICAL
- CAREER
- FAMILY
- SOCIAL
- RELATIONSHIPS

GOALS FOR BUILDING A HABIT OF GRATITUDE

- GOAL 1
- GOAL 2
- GOAL 3
- GOAL 4
- GOAL 5

count your
BLESSINGS

God is our refuge and strength, an ever-present help in trouble.

– PSALM 46:1, NIV

Date:

I'M GRATEFUL FOR:	HIGHLIGHT OF THE DAY:

Date:

I'M GRATEFUL FOR:	HIGHLIGHT OF THE DAY:

Date:

I'M GRATEFUL FOR:	HIGHLIGHT OF THE DAY:

Date:

I'M GRATEFUL FOR:	HIGHLIGHT OF THE DAY:

Date:

I'M GRATEFUL FOR:	HIGHLIGHT OF THE DAY:

Date:

I'M GRATEFUL FOR:	HIGHLIGHT OF THE DAY:

Date:

I'M GRATEFUL FOR:	HIGHLIGHT OF THE DAY:

The reflections on a day well spent furnish us with joys more pleasing than ten thousand triumphs.

– THOMAS A KEMPIS

GRATITUDE & ATTITUDE

RESPONSIBLE
OPEN MINDEDNESS JUSTICE
AUTHENTICITY
ORIGINALITY
PERSERVERANCE
COURAGE LOYALTY
CONTRIBUTION
SUPPORT UNITY FUN SERVICE

GRATITUDE & KINDNESS

♡ _____
♡ _____
♡ _____
♡ _____
♡ _____
♡ _____
♡ _____
♡ _____
♡ _____
♡ _____
♡ _____

gratitude jar

♥ _____
♥ _____
♥ _____
♥ _____
♥ _____
♥ _____
♥ _____
♥ _____

GRATITUDE & GROWTH

EMOTIONAL

PHYSICAL

CAREER

FAMILY

SOCIAL

RELATIONSHIPS

GOALS FOR BUILDING
A HABIT OF GRATITUDE

GOAL 1

GOAL 2

GOAL 3

GOAL 4

GOAL 5

count your
BLESSINGS

Give thanks to the Lord, for he is good!
His faithful love endures forever.

– PSALM 107:1, NLT

Date:

I'M GRATEFUL FOR:	HIGHLIGHT OF THE DAY:

Date:

I'M GRATEFUL FOR:	HIGHLIGHT OF THE DAY:

Date:

I'M GRATEFUL FOR:	HIGHLIGHT OF THE DAY:

Date:

I'M GRATEFUL FOR:	HIGHLIGHT OF THE DAY:

Date:

I'M GRATEFUL FOR:	HIGHLIGHT OF THE DAY:

Date:

I'M GRATEFUL FOR:	HIGHLIGHT OF THE DAY:

Date:

I'M GRATEFUL FOR:	HIGHLIGHT OF THE DAY:

What most of all hinders heavenly consolation is that you are too slow in turning yourself to prayer.

– THOMAS A KEMPIS

GRATITUDE & ATTITUDE

LEARNING **LEAD** SENSITIVITY GRATITUDE
ADVENTURE CONTENTMENT **GROWTH** PACIFIST **DREAM**
COMPASSION **ACCEPTANCE** **DEVOTION** SPONTANEOUS INTUITION
GENEROSITY **FREEDOM** INTIMACY HONESTY LISTENING HOPE **DEVOTION** FAIRNESS
COMMUNITY DEPENDABLE **WEALTH** **BEAUTY**
FRIENDLINESS

GRATITUDE & KINDNESS

♡ _____
♡ _____
♡ _____
♡ _____
♡ _____
♡ _____
♡ _____
♡ _____
♡ _____
♡ _____
♡ _____

gratitude jar

♡ _____
♡ _____
♡ _____
♡ _____
♡ _____
♡ _____
♡ _____
♡ _____

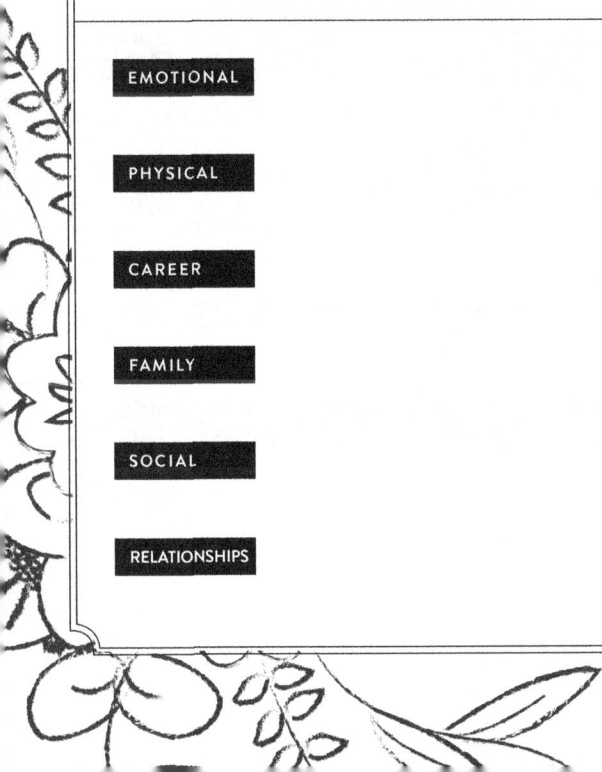

GRATITUDE & GROWTH

- EMOTIONAL
- PHYSICAL
- CAREER
- FAMILY
- SOCIAL
- RELATIONSHIPS

GOALS FOR BUILDING A HABIT OF GRATITUDE

- GOAL 1
- GOAL 2
- GOAL 3
- GOAL 4
- GOAL 5

count your
BLESSINGS

*Always be full of joy in the Lord.
I say it again - rejoice!*

– PHILIPPIANS 4:4, NLT

Date:

I'M GRATEFUL FOR:	HIGHLIGHT OF THE DAY:

Date:

I'M GRATEFUL FOR:	HIGHLIGHT OF THE DAY:

Date:

I'M GRATEFUL FOR:	HIGHLIGHT OF THE DAY:

Date:

I'M GRATEFUL FOR:	HIGHLIGHT OF THE DAY:

Date:

I'M GRATEFUL FOR:	HIGHLIGHT OF THE DAY:

Date:

I'M GRATEFUL FOR:	HIGHLIGHT OF THE DAY:

Date:

I'M GRATEFUL FOR:	HIGHLIGHT OF THE DAY:

If gratitude is due from children to their earthly parent, how much more is the gratitude of the great family of men due to our father in heaven.

– HOSEA BALLOU

GRATITUDE & ATTITUDE

SELF DEVELOPMENT
SELF RELIANCE
BALANCE
CREATIVITY
NURTURING
ATTENTIVE
LOVE
IDEALISM
RELIABLE
SECURITY
POSITIVITY
HEALTH
GRACE
FAMILY
FAITH
RISK TAKING
ENTHUSIASM
INSPIRATION
CONNECTION
TRUSTWORTHINESS
RESILIENCE
NURTURING

GRATITUDE & KINDNESS

♡ _____
♡ _____
♡ _____
♡ _____
♡ _____
♡ _____
♡ _____
♡ _____
♡ _____
♡ _____
♡ _____

gratitude jar

GRATITUDE & GROWTH

EMOTIONAL

PHYSICAL

CAREER

FAMILY

SOCIAL

RELATIONSHIPS

GOALS FOR BUILDING
A HABIT OF GRATITUDE

GOAL 1

GOAL 2

GOAL 3

GOAL 4

GOAL 5

count your
BLESSINGS

Though you have not seen him, you love him; and even though you do not see him now, you believe in him and are filled with an inexpressible and glorious joy, for you are receiving the end result of your faith, the salvation of your souls.

— 1 PETER 1:8-9, NIV

Date:

I'M GRATEFUL FOR:	HIGHLIGHT OF THE DAY:

Date:

I'M GRATEFUL FOR:	HIGHLIGHT OF THE DAY:

Date:

I'M GRATEFUL FOR:	HIGHLIGHT OF THE DAY:

Date:

I'M GRATEFUL FOR:	HIGHLIGHT OF THE DAY:

Date:

I'M GRATEFUL FOR:	HIGHLIGHT OF THE DAY:

Date:

I'M GRATEFUL FOR:	HIGHLIGHT OF THE DAY:

Date:

I'M GRATEFUL FOR:	HIGHLIGHT OF THE DAY:

Feel for others -
in your pocket.

– CHARLES SPURGEON

GRATITUDE & ATTITUDE	GRATITUDE & KINDNESS
UNDERSTANDING INTEGRITY WISDOM HUMUOR SUCCESS PEACEFUL CONTROL DEDICATION HAPPINESS DISCIPLINED INVENTIVE IMAGINATION PLAYFULNESS INTENTIONAL EQUALITY CONNECTION ENDURANCE LAUGHTER PATIENCE AWARENESS	♡ _____ ♡ _____ ♡ _____ ♡ _____ ♡ _____ ♡ _____ ♡ _____ ♡ _____ ♡ _____ ♡ _____ ♡ _____

gratitude jar

♡ _____
♡ _____
♡ _____
♡ _____
♡ _____
♡ _____
♡ _____
♡ _____

GRATITUDE & GROWTH

EMOTIONAL

PHYSICAL

CAREER

FAMILY

SOCIAL

RELATIONSHIPS

GOALS FOR BUILDING
A HABIT OF GRATITUDE

GOAL 1

GOAL 2

GOAL 3

GOAL 4

GOAL 5

count your
BLESSINGS

So now, our God, we thank You.
We praise Your great and honored name.

− 1 CHRONICLES 29:13, NLV

Date:

I'M GRATEFUL FOR:	HIGHLIGHT OF THE DAY:

Date:

I'M GRATEFUL FOR:	HIGHLIGHT OF THE DAY:

Date:

I'M GRATEFUL FOR:	HIGHLIGHT OF THE DAY:

Date:

I'M GRATEFUL FOR:	HIGHLIGHT OF THE DAY:

Date:

I'M GRATEFUL FOR:	HIGHLIGHT OF THE DAY:

Date:

I'M GRATEFUL FOR:	HIGHLIGHT OF THE DAY:

Date:

I'M GRATEFUL FOR:	HIGHLIGHT OF THE DAY:

The prayer that begins with trustfulness, and passes on into waiting, will always end in thankfulness, Triumph, and praise.

– ALEXANDER MACLAREN

GRATITUDE & ATTITUDE

RESPONSIBLE
OPEN MINDEDNESS JUSTICE
AUTHENTICITY ORIGINALITY PERSERVERANCE COURAGE LOYALTY CONTRIBUTION
SUPPORT UNITY FUN SERVICE

GRATITUDE & KINDNESS

gratitude jar

♡ _____
♡ _____
♡ _____
♡ _____
♡ _____
♡ _____
♡ _____
♡ _____

GRATITUDE & GROWTH

- EMOTIONAL
- PHYSICAL
- CAREER
- FAMILY
- SOCIAL
- RELATIONSHIPS

GOALS FOR BUILDING
A HABIT OF GRATITUDE

- GOAL 1
- GOAL 2
- GOAL 3
- GOAL 4
- GOAL 5

count your
BLESSINGS

*Until now you have not asked for anything in my name.
Ask and you will receive, and your joy will be complete.*

– JOHN 16:24, NIV

Date:

I'M GRATEFUL FOR:	HIGHLIGHT OF THE DAY:

Date:

I'M GRATEFUL FOR:	HIGHLIGHT OF THE DAY:

Date:

I'M GRATEFUL FOR:	HIGHLIGHT OF THE DAY:

Date:

I'M GRATEFUL FOR:	HIGHLIGHT OF THE DAY:

Date:

I'M GRATEFUL FOR:	HIGHLIGHT OF THE DAY:

Date:

I'M GRATEFUL FOR:	HIGHLIGHT OF THE DAY:

Date:

I'M GRATEFUL FOR:	HIGHLIGHT OF THE DAY:

There's no use doing a kindness if you do it a day too late.

— CHARLES KINGSLEY

GRATITUDE & ATTITUDE

GRATITUDE
LEARNING LEAD GROWTH PACIFIST DREAM
ADVENTURE ACCEPTANCE
COMPASSION CONTENTMENT
FREEDOM HOPE DEVOTION
WEALTH ACCEPTANCE BEAUTY FAIRNESS
FRIENDLINESS

GRATITUDE & KINDNESS

♡ _____
♡ _____
♡ _____
♡ _____
♡ _____
♡ _____
♡ _____
♡ _____
♡ _____
♡ _____
♡ _____

gratitude jar

♡ _____
♡ _____
♡ _____
♡ _____
♡ _____
♡ _____
♡ _____
♡ _____

GRATITUDE & GROWTH

EMOTIONAL

PHYSICAL

CAREER

FAMILY

SOCIAL

RELATIONSHIPS

GOALS FOR BUILDING
A HABIT OF GRATITUDE

GOAL 1

GOAL 2

GOAL 3

GOAL 4

GOAL 5

count your
BLESSINGS

Delight yourself in the Lord; and He will give you the desires of your heart.

– PSALM 37:4, NASB

Date:

I'M GRATEFUL FOR:		HIGHLIGHT OF THE DAY:

Date:

I'M GRATEFUL FOR:		HIGHLIGHT OF THE DAY:

Date:

I'M GRATEFUL FOR:		HIGHLIGHT OF THE DAY:

Date:

I'M GRATEFUL FOR:	HIGHLIGHT OF THE DAY:

Date:

I'M GRATEFUL FOR:	HIGHLIGHT OF THE DAY:

Date:

I'M GRATEFUL FOR:	HIGHLIGHT OF THE DAY:

Date:

I'M GRATEFUL FOR:	HIGHLIGHT OF THE DAY:

This way of seeing our Father in everything makes life one long thanksgiving and gives a rest of heart, and, more than that, a gayety of spirit, that is unspeakable.

– HANNAH WHITALL SMITH

GRATITUDE & ATTITUDE

SELF DEVELOPMENT
SELF RELIANCE
BALANCE
ATTENTIVE
LOVE
CREATIVITY NURTURING
IDEALISM
RELIABLE
SECURITY
POSITIVITY
HEALTH
GRACE
FAMILY
NURTURING RESILIENCE
FAITH
RISK TAKING
ENTHUSIASM
INSPIRATION
CONNECTION
TRUSTWORTHINESS

GRATITUDE & KINDNESS

gratitude jar

- ♡ _____
- ♡ _____
- ♡ _____
- ♡ _____
- ♡ _____
- ♡ _____
- ♡ _____
- ♡ _____

GRATITUDE & GROWTH

- EMOTIONAL
- PHYSICAL
- CAREER
- FAMILY
- SOCIAL
- RELATIONSHIPS

GOALS FOR BUILDING A HABIT OF GRATITUDE

- GOAL 1
- GOAL 2
- GOAL 3
- GOAL 4
- GOAL 5

count your
BLESSINGS

Blessed are those who keep his statutes and seek him with all their heart.

– PSALM 119:2, NIV

Date:

I'M GRATEFUL FOR:	HIGHLIGHT OF THE DAY:

Date:

I'M GRATEFUL FOR:	HIGHLIGHT OF THE DAY:

Date:

I'M GRATEFUL FOR:	HIGHLIGHT OF THE DAY:

Date:

I'M GRATEFUL FOR:	HIGHLIGHT OF THE DAY:

Date:

I'M GRATEFUL FOR:	HIGHLIGHT OF THE DAY:

Date:

I'M GRATEFUL FOR:	HIGHLIGHT OF THE DAY:

Date:

I'M GRATEFUL FOR:	HIGHLIGHT OF THE DAY:

Every charitable act is a stepping stone toward heaven.

– HENRY WARD BEECHER

GRATITUDE & ATTITUDE

UNDERSTANDING INTEGRITY
HUMUOR SUCCESS PEACEFUL CONTROL WISDOM
DEDICATION HAPPINESS DISCIPLINED INVENTIVE
IMAGINATION
PLAYFULNESS INTENTIONAL
EQUALITY CONNECTION ENDURANCE LAUGHTER
PATIENCE AWARENESS

GRATITUDE & KINDNESS

- ♡ _____
- ♡ _____
- ♡ _____
- ♡ _____
- ♡ _____
- ♡ _____
- ♡ _____
- ♡ _____
- ♡ _____
- ♡ _____
- ♡ _____

gratitude jar

- ♥ _____
- ♥ _____
- ♥ _____
- ♥ _____
- ♥ _____
- ♥ _____
- ♥ _____
- ♥ _____

GRATITUDE & GROWTH

- EMOTIONAL
- PHYSICAL
- CAREER
- FAMILY
- SOCIAL
- RELATIONSHIPS

GOALS FOR BUILDING A HABIT OF GRATITUDE

- GOAL 1
- GOAL 2
- GOAL 3
- GOAL 4
- GOAL 5

count your
BLESSINGS

I will sacrifice a thank offering to you and call on the name of the Lord.

– PSALM 116:17, NIV

Date:

I'M GRATEFUL FOR:	HIGHLIGHT OF THE DAY:

Date:

I'M GRATEFUL FOR:	HIGHLIGHT OF THE DAY:

Date:

I'M GRATEFUL FOR:	HIGHLIGHT OF THE DAY:

Date:

I'M GRATEFUL FOR:	HIGHLIGHT OF THE DAY:

Date:

I'M GRATEFUL FOR:	HIGHLIGHT OF THE DAY:

Date:

I'M GRATEFUL FOR:	HIGHLIGHT OF THE DAY:

Date:

I'M GRATEFUL FOR:	HIGHLIGHT OF THE DAY:

Be not afraid of rowing slowly.
Be afraid of standing still.

– HANNAH WHITALL SMITH

GRATITUDE & ATTITUDE

UNDERSTANDING INTEGRITY
HUMUOR SUCCESS PEACEFUL CONTROL WISDOM
DEDICATION HAPPINESS DISCIPLINED INVENTIVE
IMAGINATION INTENTIONAL
PLAYFULNESS CONNECTION ENDURANCE
EQUALITY LAUGHTER
PATIENCE AWARENESS

GRATITUDE & KINDNESS

♡ _____
♡ _____
♡ _____
♡ _____
♡ _____
♡ _____
♡ _____
♡ _____
♡ _____
♡ _____
♡ _____

gratitude jar

♡ _____
♡ _____
♡ _____
♡ _____
♡ _____
♡ _____
♡ _____
♡ _____

GRATITUDE & GROWTH

EMOTIONAL

PHYSICAL

CAREER

FAMILY

SOCIAL

RELATIONSHIPS

GOALS FOR BUILDING
A HABIT OF GRATITUDE

GOAL 1

GOAL 2

GOAL 3

GOAL 4

GOAL 5

Made in the USA
Middletown, DE
16 February 2023